RULES

Shaping Behavior and Knowledge

RULES

Shaping Behavior and Knowledge

FIRST EDITION

by Ronald G. Ross

Co-Founder & Principal, Business Rule Solutions, LLC
Executive Editor, BRCommunity.com
Chair, Building Business Capability (BBC) Conference

RULES

Shaping Behavior and Knowledge

FIRST EDITION

by Ronald G. Ross

ISBN 978-0-941049-20-7

To

All the wonderful teachers in my life and dedicated teachers everywhere.

Acknowledgements for the First Edition

I would like to give special thanks for ideas and feedback from the following people who gave most generously of their time and knowledge:

Don Baisley
Mike Bennett
Charlotte Bouvy
Eric Brown
Antonio Catalá Cervera
Martin Clausen
Pierre-Loic Doulcet
Jacob Feldman
Alan Fish
Denis Gagné
Patrick Grässle
Alex Hamilton
Keri Anderson Healy
Anna Lam
Gladys S.W. Lam
Vanessa Lam
Jasmine Lee
David Lyalin
Gilles Morin
Lyria Bennett Moses
Bas van der Raadt
Adrian Reed
Russell Blair Ross
Markus Schacher
Kim Schilling
Fred Simkin
Silvie Spreeuwenberg
Peter Still
Amir de la Torre
Jan Vanthienen
Matthew Waddington
Pim Willemstein

Table of Contents

Preface 1
Part I. About Rules 7
Chapter I-1. What Rules Do for Us 9
Chapter I-2. What Rules Are 17
Chapter I-3. The Two Fundamental Kinds of Rules 25
Chapter I-4. About Violations of Behavioral Rules 35
Chapter I-5. About Definitional Rules: What Counts? 45
Part II. Expressing Rules 53
Chapter II-1. Being Practicable 55
Chapter II-2. Being Declarative 61
Chapter II-3. Being Factual 67
Chapter II-4. Being Complete 73
Chapter II-5. Being Unambiguous 79
Part III. Analyzing Rules 89
Chapter III-1. Discovery of Rules 91
Chapter III-2. Discovery of Flash Points 101
Chapter III-3. Discovery of Messages 109
Part IV. Rule Quality 123
Chapter IV-1. Exceptions 125
Chapter IV-2. Anomalies 135
Chapter IV-3. Knock-Out Rules 147
Part V. Permissions, Authorizations, and Rights 155
Chapter V-1. Permissions 157
Chapter V-2. Authorizations 165
Chapter V-3. Rights 173
Conclusion: Rule Platforms in Business & Government 183

Appendix A. Concept Model Diagram for Factual Expression of Rules 191
Appendix B. Ensuring Logical Consistency of Guidance 193
Appendix C. About Decision Tables 197
Appendix D. A Word About 'Decision' 203
Appendix E. Concept Models and Their Representation 207
Appendix F. Modalities: Forms of Guidance 211
Appendix G. Positive Reinforcement and Rewards 215
Appendix H. Sample Enforcement Levels for Behavioral Rules 217
Appendix I. Warranties 221
Appendix J. Usage Constraints for Applicability Conditions 223
Appendix K. Why Not Use IF-THEN Syntax 225
Appendix L. The Relationship of Facts and Data 229
Appendix M. Structural Forms of Expression for Rules 231
Appendix N. Use of 'WHEN' 233
Appendix O. Flash Points and Definitional Rules 237
Appendix P. Eliminating Programmer Workload for Rules 241
Appendix Q. Definitions, Rules, and Logical Implications 245
Glossary 251
Index 269

Preface

For the longest time I've been encouraged by family, friends, and colleagues to write down what I've learned about rules over a lifetime of hands-on consulting, research, and standards work. So, I did. This book distills much of what I know, in what is intended to be a highly-readable form.

Although not a guidebook, the treatment is pragmatic rather than philosophical. I believe you can benefit from it, no matter what your professional orientation.

What This Book Is About

This book is about rules in human activity, especially business and government. It is not a book about symbolic AI, or about mimicking human intelligence in any form. It is not about inferencing or decision-making either, at least not directly.

Instead, this book is about rules for governing; that is, about coordinating groups or communities of people who must live and work together where risks are very real. (I'm sure that includes your organization!) The focus is on behavior and behavioral rules, whether automated or not, and on violations of those rules. It also focuses on the rights that behavioral rules confer on parties, whether in contracts and agreements or otherwise.

This orientation makes the book quite different from most of what has been written about rules in the past. It is not about exploring the frontiers of machine intelligence in academia or Silicon Valley.

Instead, it is about what real organizations need every day in analyzing and automating explicit guidance for their business, including policy, legal obligations, and deep differentiating knowledge. In that regard, it is very practical and down to earth; all about better rules for business and government.

Another way this book is different is that it focuses on natural language and its semantics. How else can groups and communities of people formally organize and manage themselves?! In that sense you can consider this book the ultimate push-back against black-box algorithms in any area of human activity where they don't belong. And there are quite a few such areas!

In that respect the book is probably more akin to legal practices and training than to the software engineering and scientific discipline of artificial intelligence (AI). In other words, rules for groups and communities of people are first and foremost a communication problem, *not* an engineering problem.

But no worries, this book is *not* about becoming a lawyer! It simply recognizes that the law has had centuries to develop patterns of thinking and practices relevant to governing and to coordinating groups and communities of people. Also, the skills definitely overlap – close reading, critical thinking, and careful writing. What policy interpreter or business analyst *doesn't* need those skills?!

It all boils down to this. Rules and rule analysis are a vital area of competency for business and government. This book provides a solid foundation for fully developing and supporting that competency.

The Current State of Rules

After so many years working with rules, I've come to a realization. Most people understand rules intuitively, but many fail to understand them well enough to work with them effectively.

Let me clarify. Governments certainly know what rules are (although perhaps not in a formal or computable sense). And those parts of business that must deal with governments and with other legal matters are fairly clear about them too (although again, not formally). How could they not be? It's been said that rules (the law) are the operating system of society.

What about business analysts, requirements professionals, and software developers? Do they understand rules well enough? With a few exceptions, not even close. I've spent countless hours trying to explain that rules and requirements are not the same thing. Requirements for automated solutions are often *based on* rules, but that's by no means the same. Unfortunately, many have been badly misled in that regard.

What about the software industry? I'm absolutely certain the software industry does *not* understand what rules for business and government are about. How can I be so sure? Because it still simply has not delivered the right platforms to support them. Without the right tooling, it is hardly a surprise that most business analysts, requirements professionals, and software developers are not clear about rules either.

Look at the evidence. The overwhelming majority of rules for business and government are still implemented using procedural software languages not at all built for that purpose.

That simply won't do. For one thing, it's not agile in the least. For another, it doesn't come even close to real-time insertion of sentiment, human discretion, and common sense in everyday activity. It's also woefully inadequate for situational sensitivity and situational awareness. And it's obviously not working for data quality. So, this book is about closing a huge current hole (read *opportunity!*) in current software platforms.

These days interest in rules arises in unexpected areas of the industry. Digital contracts anyone? Better know about rules! Better governance? Recent developments in Rules As Code and Law As Code are interesting, though not yet much known outside law and government circles.

Although you'll find almost everything in this book mostly just common sense, current platforms do not work this way. Direct support for key features of rules for groups and communities of people, especially violations, is simply missing. I hope this book will inspire much-needed innovation in software platforms.

Who This Book Is For

That said, this book is mostly for practitioners. Which practitioners? Here's a partial list of all the professionals who need to truly understand rules.

- Policy Maker
- Policy Advisor
- Policy Interpreter
- Legislative Drafter
- Rule Maker
- Rule Analyst
- Regulator
- Compliance Officer
- Legal Staff
- Contract Drafter
- Auditor
- Risk Analyst
- Decision Modeler
- Business Analyst
- Requirements Engineer
- Product Owner
- Data Quality Professional
- Data Governance Professional
- Business Process Manager
- Business Process Analyst
- Business System Analyst
- Business Software Developer

If your role or responsibility involves one or more of the above, I believe you'll find a treasure trove of practical ideas you can apply in your daily responsibilities.

In addition, I believe this material should be studied in universities, business schools, and law schools. Being rule-based is the most basic characteristic of Western civilization. These core ideas should be taught as widely as possible.

If you want to deeply understand rules for business and government, you've come to the right place. Here's how to be rule-based about anything involving groups and communities of people, including their knowledge!

Notes to the Reader

- All core terms used in this book are defined in the Glossary, which should be used as a helpful reference.
- The most fundamental of these core terms are illustrated diagrammatically in Appendix A, showing key structural relationships. Do have a quick look.
- The book includes over a dozen Appendices. These allow the main text to remain as short as possible, while providing an opportunity for those interested to dig deeper on selected topics.

Additional Reading

1. Rules being independent of processes and procedures is a fundamental idea of the *Business Rules Manifesto: The Principles of Rule Independence*, 2003. The 2-page, easy-to-read Manifesto expresses fundamental ideas of this book, including the connection to knowledge. It has been translated into 17 languages. https://www.brcommunity.com/articles.php?id=s030
2. Our methods and techniques were used for the Better Rules Initiative in New Zealand: *Better Rules for Government Discovery Report* – Better Rules for Government Discovery Report | NZ Digital government https://www.digital.govt.nz/dmsdocument/95-better-rules-for-government-discovery-report/html
3. The Better Rules Initiative was the starting point for the OECD's *Cracking the Code: Rulemaking for Humans and Machines* – https://www.oecd.org/innovation/cracking-the-code-3afe6ba5-en.htm
4. The content of this book is consistent with, and grounded in, the Object Management Group (OMG) specification *Semantics of Business Vocabulary and Business Rules* (SBVR), which in turn is grounded in predicate logic. For more about SBVR see the *SBVR Insider* section on www.BRCommunity.com

Part I

About Rules

The most basic questions about rules are *what* and *why*. What exactly are rules, and why do you need them? This first Part explains. You might be in for some surprises.

Beyond that you need to know what kinds of rules there are and why it makes a difference. Surprisingly there are two and only two fundamental kinds of rules – but they are worlds apart. Specifically, some rules can be violated and some cannot.

- Rules that people and organizations can violate directly shape behavior. They are fundamental to living and working in groups and communities of people.
- Rules that cannot be violated define concepts, shape our knowledge, and allow us to count things precisely. Those things are important too.

Does it come as any surprise to you that many rules can be broken? It shouldn't – look around you in the real world. Rules are broken *all the time!*

Unfortunately, most current approaches to interpreting guidance, designing business solutions, and analyzing business knowledge never focus on violations directly. How could that be right?! So, instead of dancing all around the inconvenient fact that rules can be broken, we should entertain it directly. We need to become *violations-aware.*

Instead of dancing all around the inconvenient fact that rules can be broken, we should entertain it directly.

RULES

This part of the book will arm you with all the basic insights about rules you need to move toward a rule-based approach and, in the process, create an agile, real-time enterprise.

Chapter I-1

What Rules Do for Us

In 2005, I broke two basic rules of responsible ladder usage:

- Never stand on the top rung of a ladder.
- Never use a ladder alone.

I paid a hefty price – a broken right arm and a stay in the hospital the night before a hurricane was supposed to hit my home town. (Yes, my ill-advised ladder usage and the looming hurricane were related.)

The incident was also a teaching moment. Ladders are more dangerous than you might imagine. You can bet I have never violated those rules since! (And now I can hope you won't either.) Wrapped up in those rules is important knowledge that can be passed on to others' advantage. Better to learn dangerous things through rules than personal experience(!).

In general, rules are potent teaching tools. Actually, rules and knowledge are inseparable. If you want to communicate and retain knowledge, rules are of the essence. So, in the Knowledge Age it's important to understand them more than just intuitively.

Rules and knowledge are inseparable.

Rules and Risks

As my ladder episode indicates, one fundamental purpose of rules is to protect against significant risks. They provide markers of known dangers, guardrails against counterproductive behavior. Good ones tend to keep you on safe, productive paths.

In a day and age of increasingly dynamic or unscripted behaviors, guardrails and rules of engagement are ever more essential. That's all the more true for artificial intelligence (AI) since it has no innate biological or cultural constraints.

Rules and Community

See if you recognize the following children's game from just the rules:

1. Players must walk in single file around a group of chairs while music plays.
2. Each player must sit in a chair when the music stops.
3. A player not sitting in a chair when the music stops must be eliminated from the game.
4. One chair must be removed each time the music restarts.
5. A player is considered the winner of the game if they are the only player sitting in a chair when the music stops.

The game, of course, is musical chairs.

Can you imagine any game without a set of rules? Where there is a group or community of people, and it seeks some common purpose or goal, there will always be rules in some form. Rules are how you create order from disorder. That's what laws, statutes, regulations, contracts, agreements, etc. are all about. Rules are also how you remember things and avoid unconscious biases and discrimination (perhaps in machine learning as well).

Rules are how you create order from disorder.

Rules and Governance

Policies are basic to the working of governance. Policies shape the broad contours of desired behavior within or across communities of people. Associated with policy are sanctions, either positive ones to reward desired behavior or negative ones to discourage undesired behavior.

Policies generally must be interpreted to apply at the fine-grained level of everyday group behavior. What do you get when you interpret policies? *Rules*. If you create policies someone –

maybe you, maybe someone else – will also be creating rules. Along with penalties and incentives, policies and rules represent the gear box of governance.

Policies and rules represent the gear box of governance.

Besides policies, institutional knowledge also involves norms (often tacit) and practices and procedures (sometimes formalized, sometimes not). These too can be rich sources of rules highly relevant to some or all of the community.

Rules and Government

A specific government or regulatory body actually has multiple relationships with rules. This book applies to each.

- Rules *in* government. The government or regulatory body, like a business, creates and applies rules for its own activities.
- Rules *by* government. The body is a producer of rules (in the form of legislation or regulations) that apply to some or all parties who thereby become consumers of the rules. For example, no one is allowed to assault another party. Some rules are selective to parties, for example those organizations in a certain industry sector. Consumption in that case is the stuff of regulatory compliance.

  Aside: Terminology varies, but in rules by government, policy makers (e.g., congress or parliament) 'make' rules, assisted by policy advisors (officials of various stripes) and legislative drafters (who write actual rule statements).

Rules and Innovation

These days innovation is top of everyone's mind. Many shout mindlessly "break all the rules!" as if doing so will cure all ills of stagnation. Catchy slogan but like all panaceas, simplistic and misdirected. Here's a better view.[1]

> *Clear, predictable rules protect freedom of action as much as constrain it. Rules determine not just what is prohibited, but also help protect what is allowed. Rules that are explicit can be incrementally improved upon.*
>
> *By contrast, failure to spell out what is and isn't allowed can have a chilling effect, in which people steer clear of innovation. Few want to risk doing things differently knowing others have been sanctioned by unpredictable authorities for overstepping invisible lines.*

In a great many cases, when people say they have too many rules what they really mean is that rules are implemented rigidly in processes and procedures that are overly complex. Or the rules are so poorly encoded as to seem voluminous. It all builds up like scar tissue. Yes, in that sense they are absolutely right – 'too many rules'!

Rules and Strategy

Thinking about rules in the context of games is instructive in another sense. To win games, you employ strategy. What does strategy do? It identifies the ends (goals and objectives) you want to achieve and the means (including policies and rules) to achieve them.[2]

But at some level, goals or objectives always conflict. If you go too far in one direction to satisfy some goal(s), you can easily undercut your ability to achieve some other goal(s). At its heart,

---

1 Based on two paragraphs from "Free Speech's New Frontier," *The Economist*, Feb 5, 2022, p. 13-14, paraphrased, reworded, and generalized.

2 Policies and rules are a recognized key component of strategy. Refer to *The Business Motivation Model* (BMM) by the Business Rules Group, 2000. https://www.brcommunity.com/brg/BRG-BMM.pdf In 2010, BMM was released as an Object Management Group (OMG) specification.

strategy is about establishing optimal compromises between conflicting goals so as to ensure highest chances of success.

How do you express those compromises? By establishing policies and developing rules. Here's a simple example. Suppose order fulfillment in a business has three business goals:

Goal 1: To stay competitive.

Goal 2: To keep customers satisfied.

Goal 3: To make a profit.

The business decides to accept orders on credit as part of its strategy. Doing so will help it (1) stay competitive and (2) keep customers satisfied. But there's a risk: Non-payment of purchases made on credit. Since the business also needs (3) to make a profit, how does it protect itself? How far is it willing to go to achieve the first two goals at risk of the third? To resolve the conflict, it establishes the following rule:

Orders on credit over $1000 should not be accepted without a credit check.

The motivation for most policies and rules is seldom worked out as explicitly as this, but dig deep enough and you will always find risk and conflict resolution. (If you can't, you might question why you need the policy in the first place.)

Rules and Customer Experience

The only thing worse than a consistently bad customer experience, is an inconsistently bad one. With a consistent experience, you expect it. When it's inconsistent you don't know what to expect!

How do you ensure consistent customer experience? Rules. Not just rules applied consistently at one touch point, but rules applied consistently across all collaborations and all channels (both digital and in-person) through which parties interact. And to the data on which all the interactions depend.

Rules can ensure consistent experience.

Rules and Concepts

As earlier, rules often pertain directly to behavior. They can also relate indirectly to behavior, by helping to shape the understanding on which behavior is based. Specifically, many rules provide definitional criteria. To illustrate, let's return to the game of musical chairs. The fifth rule from earlier determines the winner of the game:

> *A player is considered the winner of the game if they are the only player sitting in a chair when the music stops.*

The term 'winner' should have a definition, of course, but the rule above is almost certainly not part of that definition. The rule is supplemental to the definition, providing criteria to determine which person can be classified as the winner.

That's a child's game, of course, so the criterion is simple. But consider the complex concepts we deal with in real life – e.g., 'market share', 'restricted air space', 'freedom of speech', 'money-back guarantee', etc. Each of these concepts could have many dozens of qualifying definitional criteria.

Your knowledge is not complete until you make those definitional criteria explicit as rules. Otherwise, you will sometimes use the concepts incorrectly – not only disrupting business activity but likely producing bad data as well.

Rules and Inference

A special case of definitional criteria are rules that support what is commonly called inference, rules that infer new facts from existing facts. They too are an important form of knowledge-building rules. Here is a simple classic example:

If it is raining, then streets are wet.

The fact of wet streets is the logical implication of the fact of rain happening.

> *Aside:* Just because an inference can be made in one direction does not necessarily mean it can be made in the other direction. For example, you can't assume 'If streets are wet, then it is raining'. A watermain might have burst, the city might be washing the streets, etc.

Such inference rules are the prominent feature of traditional expert systems (non-statistical AI). They are often strung together (chained) in order to make more sophisticated determinations.

In the past decade, machine learning has proven far more powerful for many forms of intelligent behavior than expert systems, so inferencing has fallen into disfavor for many kinds of bots. One important exception has arisen in business, however – the automation of operational business decisions using decision models and decision tables.

Actually, there's no surprise there. You'll always resort to explicit rules whenever you want both the following:

- Consistency of results no matter what the process.
- Traceability – being able to explain the 'why' of results.

You'll always resort to explicit rules whenever you want to be able to explain the 'why' of results.

Rules and Requirements

Rules provide the basic motivation for many requirements. Suppose I say, "We need a piano." Would you have any idea why we need the piano? How about if I also gave you the five rules from earlier for the game of musical chairs. *Then* would you know why we need a piano?

The five rules, however, actually say nothing whatsoever about pianos. The rules simply call for *music*. Instead of a piano, you could simply play music from an electronic device. 'Music-playing electronic device' is probably a better, more practical requirement than 'piano'.

See the difference between rules and requirements? Rules shape activity for groups and communities of people; requirements identify how you've decided to support that activity.[3] The rules will remain relevant throughout the life of the activity; the original requirements much less so after implementation.

To use rules in automation projects, do you have to know all the rules upfront? Well, yes you should – *if* we're talking about contractual or other legal constraints. Otherwise, of course not! You live and learn.

The goal is to develop the rules for an activity such that they are shared, retained, and accessible for the whole community. And, of course, revisable – because the rules *will* change over time.

Rules and Data

The connection between rules and data is actually simple. The results of business activity are recorded as data. So, rules for business are also actually rules for data. Not a different set of rules, but the very *same* rules!

Rules for business and rules for data are the very same rules.

If you want high data quality, ultimately the best and perhaps only way to get there is through rules applied in real time with respect to business activity. Want to understand more? *Read on.*

---

3 Certain requirements can be developed directly from rules. In that case the rules provide the requirements' motivation. Rules can also be used in assessing the completeness of requirements. These important topics, however, are outside the scope of this book.

Chapter I-2

What Rules Are

For groups and communities of people, a rule is a guide for conduct or action. Its expression provides criteria for judging or evaluating that conduct or action. In other words, a rule serves as a criterion for making judgments and decisions. Consider this simple example posted on a sign at the entrance to a restaurant near the beach.

Rule: *No shirt, no service.*

Using the criterion 'no shirt', a decision can be made (by the restaurant, the customer, or anyone else) about someone dining at that restaurant.

As this example suggests, a rule tends to remove a degree of freedom. (I say 'tends to' because actual results depend on how strictly the rule is enforced.) You can dine in lots of places but, without a shirt, not at *that* restaurant. A rule always tends to *constrain* in the sense of narrowing ('ruling out') options or contingencies.

A rule tends to remove some degree of freedom.

Rules, States, and Actions

Rules and actions are different, fundamentally and unconditionally. If you let the distinction between the two become hazy, your logic is likely to become hazy too.

- By *action*, I mean performing, doing, or transforming something. In the example above, the act of entering the restaurant as a customer is an action.

The important thing about actions is that they can change the state of things. Before an action, the world is in one state; after an action, the world can be in a different state.

Aside: This is true even for an unsuccessful action – for example, a potential customer being rejected at the restaurant for lack of a shirt. The state of the world has changed because now there is knowledge of at least the unsuccessful action itself. Even if the potential customer didn't get in, they tried.

- *Rules*, in contrast, are not actions, and not really even *about* actions, at least not directly. For example, the No Shirt, No Service Rule doesn't imply any action on its own. Instead, it's simply a criterion for whether service can be properly given and received.

  Directly, rules are always about the states of things (or more precisely, states of affairs), not actions. The rule above disallows shirtless customers – in other words, it disallows the state of the restaurant in which some shirtless customer is served.

Rules are always about the states of things, not actions directly.

As another example, consider the action *Take Rental Car Reservation* at a car rental company. If successful, the action will leave the world in a new state. Specifically, a reservation holder will hold a reservation that they did not have before. To be successful, however, the action must leave the world in a state that complies with relevant rules, for example:

Reservation Rules	A reservation always requests a car group.
	A reservation must indicate an intended pick-up branch.
	The reservation holder of a points reservation must be a club member.

In summary, actions do things to try to change the state of the world. Rules, in contrast, simply indicate which states of the world are:

- correct or incorrect
- allowed or disallowed
- legal or illegal
- obligated or prohibited
- necessary or impossible

Applying Rules

As above, actions always try to change states. Rules, in contrast, pertain to the new states that actions seek to create. If the new state is acceptable, there is no need for intervention. If not acceptable, intervention should happen to prevent an undesirable state, ideally in real time. For example, a shirtless person who seeks to dine is turned away at the entrance into the restaurant.

Rules should ideally be applied in real time to prevent undesirable states.

Unfortunately, such timely intervention is not always possible. Consider the Commandment *Thou shalt not kill.* Unfortunately, murder often cannot be prevented. Victims *do* die; the rule is sometimes broken.

What is the role of rules in such cases?

- Before the action, the rule sets expectations for behavior. Not murdering is expected of all members of the community.
- After the action, the rule provides the criteria for assessing wrongness. Although the wrong state (a dead victim) could not be prevented, the violation certainly can be detected and should be penalized in appropriate fashion.

Rules, Actions, and Inferences

Inference rules might seem to muddle the distinction between actions and rules. *No!*

First of all, an inference 'rule' that calls for execution of an action is not a rule at all. Rather, it is an instruction, no matter what some software platform calls it. Consider this example:

Sign Posted on Glass Box Containing an Ax: *In case of fire, break glass.*

This statement is conditional ("in case of fire") but gives an instruction ("break glass"). It calls for the execution of an action. It is not a rule.

Aside: Maintaining the distinction between rules and actions is critical. Restricting rules to state creates a guidance knowledgebase (rulebook) with clear boundaries within which consistency can be logically verified. Invoking actions can have unknown consequences (side effects). Strict separation of concerns is therefore essential. For more, refer to Appendix B.

So, let's restrict ourselves to inference rules that imply facts from other facts, for example:

Rule: *If raining, then streets are wet.*

No matter what happens under the covers in some platform, the inferred fact always exists as soon as the conditional fact is true. Nothing 'made' it true; it's simply true that streets are wet if it is raining. Period.

With decision models and decision tables (refer to Appendix C), it may look like there's an action (task) that produces some new outcome, but that's simply a choice some process or application designer has made about when to look at the results of the inferencing. (Many operational business decisions can be optimized by waiting as long 'to look' as possible.) Logically, the inferred facts (inferences) were there all the time – just not looked at. Refer to Appendix D for an important word of caution about 'decision'.

Expressing Knowledge of States

The language of actions is very different from the language of rules. To specify an action, generally you use verbs as commands. (In natural language, such specification uses verbs in the imperative mood.) For example:

- *Do X*
- *Build X*
- *Use X*
- *Sell X*
- *Buy X*
- *Perform X*
- *Read X*

These commands can become quite complex and can involve a great many Xs. The Xs, of course, are all labeled, sometimes (but by no means always) with business-friendly labels. The emphasis, however, is on getting things done – that is, on instructions – not on organizing and expressing knowledge about states of the world per se.

Expressing such knowledge also requires many Xs – terms for all the business things of interest. And it requires verbs to relate those things as well – but never in the command form. Instead, knowledge about states of the world is always expressed as facts. Here are some examples, using the same verbs from above:

- People **do** yoga in the park.
- Beachgoers **build** sandcastles.
- Carpenters **use** hammers.
- Supermarkets **sell** spices.
- Customers **buy** emergency supplies on credit.
- Orchestras **perform** concerts.
- Parents **read** books to children at bedtime.

These are all simple facts; many are far more complex. But use of the verbs in these sentences (and yes, all facts are expressed as sentences) does not impel any action. When we communicate knowledge about states, we use verbs simply to express structural relations between the Xs.

> *Aside:* In natural language, such specification uses verbs in the indicative mood rather than the imperative mood. Using verbs in the indicative mood expresses an action as a statement of fact.

Expressing rules about states goes one small, but important step farther. A rule doesn't express an actual fact, but rather what should or should not be a fact.

A rule doesn't express an actual fact, but rather what should or should not be a fact.

This is a very instinctive thing in natural language. Here are some examples based on several of the facts above, using the auxiliary verb *should:*

- Supermarkets **should sell** many spices.
- Customers **should not buy** emergency supplies on credit.

Voila, *rules!*

These examples illustrate how closely rules and structured natural language are woven together. For all practical purposes, they are inseparable. Yes, these are simple rules, but expressing more complex ones simply involves referencing more nouns and verbs – that is, more concepts.

Actually, the hard part of expressing any rule lies not so much with its *ruleness* per se but with expressing all the relevant concepts succinctly. The ability to express facts and rules succinctly is the purpose of a structured business vocabulary based on concept model.[4] Such a vocabulary is more than simply a 'controlled vocabulary'. Refer to Appendix E for a brief but important discussion of concept models.

By the way, to keep things simple I cheated a bit above when I used the word 'should'. There are actually two fundamental kinds of rules, and 'should' applies only to one. *More to come!*

---

4 Refer to *Business Knowledge Blueprints: Enabling Your Data to Speak the Language of the Business* (2nd ed), by Ronald G. Ross, 2020.

Chapter I-3

The Two Fundamental Kinds of Rules

Rules often pertain directly to behavior. *No Shirt, No Service.* Such rules are called *behavioral rules.* The world abounds in such rules; business and society are based on them.

Rules can also relate indirectly to behavior, by helping to shape the understanding on which behavior is based. For example, what's a 'shirt'? Does an undershirt count? How about a tank top? A bikini top? Does a shirt have to cover the shoulders? *Definitional rules* provide criteria to answer such questions.

Behavioral rules and definitional rules are fundamentally different, a fact having profound consequences for business, analysis, and software platforms. Specifically, behavioral rules can be violated (by people, organizations, or software acting in their behalf) – definitional rules can't be violated, *ever.*

Behavioral rules can be violated –
definitional rules can't be violated, ever.

Another difference is that, unlike definitional rules, behavioral rules confer *rights* in groups and communities of people. Rights are hardly a trivial matter, not least where contracts and agreements are involved. (Refer to Chapter V-3.)

Figure 1 represents the two kinds of rules. (Relevant definitions are found in the Glossary.) The heavy dark lines indicate categories.

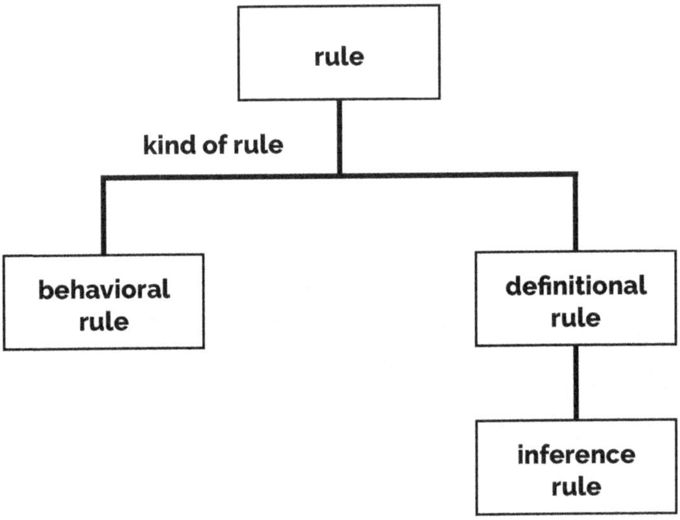

Figure 1. *The Two Fundamental Kinds of Rules*

Inference rule is shown as a special category of definitional rule. Perhaps it seems a bit lonely there under definitional rule. Appearances are deceiving. As Part V discusses, there's a rich panoply of guidance associated with behavioral rules.

Behavioral Rules vs. Definitional Rules

Think *Thou Shalt Not Kill*. Society has police forces, judicial systems, prisons, and much more, all because such behavioral rules can be violated. Seeking out and responding to violations of these rules is the very essence of compliance.

Definitional rules, in contrast, might be misunderstood, misinterpreted, or misapplied but can never be violated. Definitional rules simply shape knowledge about the world; certain concepts (e.g., 'shirt') simply are what they are *by definition*. There is no choice in the matter. (Since there is no choice in the matter, the word 'should' is inappropriate for expressing definitional rules.)

For example, if you let someone into a restaurant wearing a ragged undershirt, you didn't violate the (definitional) What's-a-Shirt Rule(s), you violated the (behavioral) No-Shirt, No-Service Rule. You merely forgot about or misunderstood the What's-a-Shirt Rule(s). (Sample rule later.) Behavioral rules, not definitional rules, are where the rubber meets the road in human activity.

Behavioral rules are where the rubber meets the road in human activity.

What are definitional rules for? Definitional rules supplement definitions. (More later on exactly how.) Definitional rules literally tell you what counts as an instance of a concept and what doesn't. For some concepts they can be numerous and complex. Examples:

- Does a case of self-defense count as a murder?
- Does a prospect count as a customer?
- Does a subsidiary's customer count toward a company's market share?

Certainly, you can have behavioral rules without definitional rules, but such behavioral rules are likely to prove less than effective. To say that differently, behavioral rules without definitional rules are often vague. Lack of precision means enforcement will be inconsistent or capricious.

Definitional rules tell you what counts as an instance of a concept and what doesn't.

How do you determine whether a rule is behavioral or definitional? Ask whether or not it always has to be true *by definition.* For example:

Rule: *A customer is to be assigned an agent if the customer has placed an order.*

Is there anything in the definitions of customer, agent, or order that requires this rule to be true in all circumstances (in logic, all possible worlds)? The answer is probably *no*. So, this is a behavioral rule. It can be broken.

More About Behavioral Rules

Behavioral rules aim to directly shape people's behavior (even when embedded in manual procedures, represented by software, or enforced by bots). Just like rules for your children, they set boundaries for acceptable behavior.

Some boundaries are meant to be hard ones: *Never run into the street without looking*. Other boundaries are meant to be soft ones: *Never pull the dog's tail*. In other words, strict adherence to some behavioral rules is expected; others serve just as guidelines.

In business, it's quite important to know which is which. Enforcement or sanction for violating 'hard' rules should be stringent; for 'soft' rules, enforcement and sanction can be relatively mild or even non-existent. Nonetheless, it's important to recognize that guidelines are rules too. All behavior-shaping rules should rest on the same footing so they can be collectively marshalled to greatest effect.

Guidelines are rules too.

Because of the direct implications for people's activity in going about their activity, behavioral rules carry the sense of *obligation* or *prohibition*. (Refer to Appendix F.) Behavioral rules indicate what:

- must or must not be
- ought or ought not be
- should or should not be

The key thing to remember about behavioral rules is that they can be violated. Their intent is to shape or constrain the actions and activity of people and organizations (actors with agency).

Aside: Such actions or activity do not include CRUD (create, retrieve, update, delete) events per se. Those are merely events in a record-keeping (data) system, not the real world of actors with agency. (Refer to Chapter III-2.) On the other hand, suppose an outside organization supplies your organization with data. That action is subject to behavioral rules because two actors with agency are involved.

Consider the following rule:

Warehouse Access Rule: *A gold customer must be given access to the warehouse.*

If a gold customer is denied access to the warehouse, then a violation has occurred. Presumably, some sanction is associated with such violation – for example, a security guard might be called on the carpet.

Aside: It is not possible or even desirable to name every rule. Rules here and elsewhere in the book are named to provide easy reference for discussion.

Since behavioral rules can be broken, their analysis needs to carefully focus on the potential for violations. The next chapter discusses five key questions for being violations-aware.

For the same reason, behavioral rules also require special care in reasoning (automated or otherwise). Consider the Warehouse Access Rule for example. It cannot be assumed that the rule has always been faithfully enforced; therefore, it cannot be inferred that in every situation where it was appropriate for a gold customer to be allowed access to the warehouse, the customer actually was allowed such access. Violations happen!

Aside: Here and elsewhere, I use 'reasoning' to mean evaluating rules to logically infer factual conclusions from other facts.

Many behavioral rules are automatable. Here are some examples:

- *An order over $1,000 must not be accepted on credit without a credit check.*
- *A high-risk customer must not place a rush order.*
- *An order's date promised must be at least 24 hours after the order's date taken.*

Some behavioral rules are not automatable, at least not directly using current technology (e.g., *No elbows on the table.*). Non-automatable behavioral rules require special attention to detecting potential and actual violations, and to enforcing consequences.

Technology is moving forward, of course, at breakneck speed. Behavioral rules formerly considered non-automatable are falling like dominos to bots and special surveillance measures. Consider the Warehouse Access Rule. Would it be feasible to use facial recognition software to admit gold customers to the warehouse while rejecting others?

More About Definitional Rules

Definitional rules also shape people's behavior, but only indirectly. Instead of behavior, they shape the concepts on which behavior is based.

Wait a second, isn't the purpose of definitions to shape concepts? Yes. The problem, however, is that definitions usually leave too much wiggle room for business purposes (and reasoning). Consider this definition of shirt[5]:

> Definition of Shirt: *a garment for the upper part of the body, as a loose cloth garment usually having a collar, sleeves, a front opening, and a tail long enough to be tucked inside the waistband of trousers or a skirt*

---

5 *Merriam-Webster Unabridged Dictionary:* (1) and (1a).

"Garment for the upper part of the body" is vague (how much of the upper body?); the word "usually" isn't helpful at all (specifically *when?!*). The definition leaves many other unanswered questions, such as whether a shirt absolutely has to have:

- a collar. (If so, t-shirts are excluded.)
- sleeves. (If so, muscle shirts are excluded.)
- a tail long enough to be tucked inside the waistband of trousers or a skirt. (If so, crop tops are excluded.)

Without some definitional rule(s) to close these gaps, who knows how the (behavioral) No-Shirt, No-Service Rule will be enforced in practice!

Let's suppose the restaurant does intend a shirt to have sleeves and a long 'tail,' but not necessarily a collar. If so, the following definitional rule needs to be specified explicitly in addition to the concept's definition:

What's-a-Shirt Rule: *A shirt has sleeves and a tail long enough to be tucked inside the waistband of trousers or a skirt.*

Instead of defining a separate rule for these conditions, could the definition itself just have been modified? *Yes*. Is that always practical? *No*. Consider how many specific criteria might be involved for concepts such as:

- murder
- money-back guarantee
- supplemental income

Definitional rules are useful where a higher degree of precision is needed than basic definitions provide because of the risks associated with misapplication of some behavioral rule(s).

Definitional rules provide precision to supplement definitions where misapplying behavioral rules is a significant risk.

Sorting out all the extensive criteria to ensure consistent interpretation and application of behavioral rules is the heart of the problem for laws, regulations, contracts, agreements, business policies, and so on. Indeed, it is the heart of the problem for deep knowledge of *any* subject matter that involves risks. All such specifics usually just don't fit comfortably in definitions.

Because of the direct relationship of definitional rules to definitions, definitional rules carry the sense of *necessity* or *impossibility*. (Refer to Appendix F.) Definitional rules indicate what:

- counts and does not count
- has to be or has not to be

The key thing to remember about definitional rules is that they *cannot* be directly violated.

Let's assume the following for 'gold customer'.

Definition of Gold Customer: *a customer that regularly places large orders and merits highest-level service*

Gold Customer Rule: *A customer is considered a gold customer if the customer places more than 12 large orders during a calendar year that are each fully paid within 60 days.*

Now remember the (behavioral) Warehouse Access Rule:

Warehouse Access Rule: *A gold customer must be given access to the warehouse.*

If a gold customer is denied access to the warehouse, it's not because definitional Gold Customer Rule has been violated; it is because the behavioral Warehouse Access Rule was violated. The former rule can only be misunderstood, misinterpreted, or misapplied.

All definitional rules are potentially automatable. Since definitional rules cannot be broken (unlike behavioral rules), definitional rules can be used directly for reasoning – automated or otherwise.

Aside: To be automatable, a rule must be practicable. (Refer to Chapter II-1.) Whether an automated definitional rule can be evaluated in real time depends on whether all the relevant facts are available.

Definitional rules are basic to asking for counts of things. Getting counts right does require some awareness of time. For example, if you had asked in 2005 how many planets our solar system has, the answer would be 9. As of this writing, the answer would be 8. Definitional rules can change over time. *Poor Pluto!*

Chapter I-4

About Violations of Behavioral Rules

The key feature of rules for groups and communities of people is that individuals and organizations (and machines) will sometimes break the rules.

It's obvious. It happens all the time. Just look around you. Think about how much time and energy we spend trying to anticipate, detect, and sanction violations. That's why we have regulators, police, and prisons. And compliance departments. And endless data cleansing activity.

People and organizations have agency; as actors they have free will. They have flaws, motivations, and insights that sometimes lead them to break the rules. It's up to the authority behind the rules (the body that creates and monitors the rules) to determine which breaches are deadly serious (murder), which are minor (jaywalking), and which are actually innovative ('thinking outside the box').

There's more. Whenever a rule is violated, some party is stepping on some other party's right. Sometimes the transgression is not worth mention; other times the harm is quite significant. To protect such rights, governments make laws and regulations, and parties enter into contracts and agreements.

Our current approaches dance all around the fact that rules can be broken – or ignore it completely. Instead, the fact that rules can be broken should be front and center. We should make the possibility of violations a centerpiece of guidance and analysis. It's the key to being rule-based, and to being a real-time enterprise as well.

The key feature of rules for groups and communities of people is that individuals and organizations (and machines) will sometimes break the rules.

Five Violation Questions for Behavioral Rules

Being violations-aware is not as hard as you might think. Once you capture the rules, the patterns are straightforward. All you need to know is what questions to ask and what form the answers can take. Specifications that before may have seemed ill-focused and incomplete now become orderly and explainable.

Table 1 lists the five questions you can ask about each behavioral rule and identifies the default answer for each question. The discussion in the rest of this chapter provides additional explanation and examples.

Table 1. Questions for Behavioral Rules

	Violation Question	Comment
1	*How are potential and actual violations detected?*	If automation is not feasible, then by human intervention. Real-time detection is highly desirable wherever feasible so the effects don't compound themselves in downstream activity.
2	*What enforcement level?*	'Strictly enforced' can be considered the default answer. The opposite extreme from strictly enforced is 'guideline'.
3	*What guidance message?*	The rule statement itself can always serve as the guidance message because the rule should precisely express the criteria from which any violation could arise. Additional or alternative messaging, however, can be specified.
4	*What special violation response?*	Special actions, processes, or procedures (always optional) that can be invoked to avoid, mitigate, sanction, or compensate for the violation.
5	*What applicability conditions?*	The same base rule can be enforced selectively for different situations or circumstances.

Some important points about these questions:

1. Since the possibility of violations is the central characteristic of behavioral rules, the questions naturally focus on violations. Detecting and rewarding *compliance* with behavioral rules, however, might sometimes also be desirable. (Who doesn't like the occasional treat for acting properly, especially when learning?!) Also, the performance of particular actor(s) in complying can be monitored over time. Refer to Appendix G for discussion.
2. How strictly you want a behavioral rule to be enforced (question 2), and what you want to do in response to violations (questions 3-4), are different issues than the logic the rule itself expresses. Separating these concerns is highly empowering.
3. Questions 3-5 are optional. They simply expand on your capacity to apply the rules intelligently.

Answers to the questions usually only emerge over time, not when a rule is first drafted. Where special answers are required, iterative walk-throughs of different scenarios always prove helpful.

Most importantly, answers should not be considered static once deployed. They should be easy to change so that reactions to violations can evolve naturally as circumstances warrant. Such capability is key to being rule-based, as well as to true business agility.

Question 1: How Are Potential and Actual Violations Detected?

How to detect violations is the most basic question of all for a behavioral rule. If violations can't be detected, then a rule cannot serve as more than as simply a guideline. That fact doesn't mean the rule isn't important; shaping behavior through education and awareness is by no means a trivial aspect of rules.

Fortunately, many behavioral rules are directly automatable, so detection is more or less a given.

> *Aside:* The "more or less" depends on available platform or software environment. Technical staff may need to analyze how potential violations can be detected using current capabilities.

For those rules that are not directly automatable given available technology, human intervention is required. Responsibility for detecting potential and actual violations must become part of someone's job responsibilities (and training).

Consider the No-Shirt, No-Service Rule. Who will be responsible for verifying shirts are being worn by customers? Consider these possibilities:

- *The restaurant has seating hosts at the entrance.* A relatively straightforward solution is to task those hosts with responsibility for detecting potential violations. A big advantage is real-time enforcement.
- *The restaurant is self-seating.* Here, the question becomes more difficult. Perhaps responsibility could be given to waiters. Or better, perhaps to a roving manager, in order to separate service from policing.
- *The restaurant is self-service (think cafeteria or server machines).* Now, the problem potentially becomes very difficult. Apparently, the restaurant was purposely designed to minimize human intervention, so the rule could be colliding with basic business strategy. Perhaps the restaurant could simply rely on the honor system (and the disdainful frowns of fellow customers). Or maybe the rule should simply be discontinued.

In examining these possibilities, did you notice (if not before) that 'service' needs defining? For example, can a customer enter without a shirt if the 'service' is simply to pick up a take-out order?

Aside: A bot at the entrance could probably support automatic shirt recognition. For the average restaurant, of course, this solution might prove too expensive or difficult. And what could the bot safely do about enforcement? Make no mistake, however, bots will increasingly be used for detection of violations where feasible and ethical. Ever get a traffic citation through the mail for late entry into an intersection at a red light? Or using a toll road without the proper windshield tag?

Question 2:
What Enforcement Level?

The most distinctive question for a behavioral rule is how strictly it should be enforced. Consider the No-Shirt, No-Service Rule. Assuming the rule is fundamental to the business strategy, it should probably be strictly enforced.

But some discretion might be warranted. Consider the following possibilities.

- The air conditioning is broken and it's quite hot inside.
- A young child barely walking is brought by properly-attired parents.
- The restaurant owner shows up shirtless and wants to dine.

Perhaps the host should be permitted to override the rule in some or all of these circumstances. Allowing for (well-considered) human discretion in the enforcement of rules in appropriate situations is a fundamental need for business and government.

Allowing for human discretion in the enforcement of rules is a fundamental need for business and government.

'Guideline' is the least restrictive of all enforcement levels (no sanction of any kind for violation). Essentially a guideline is simply a well-formed suggestion. Still, a guideline should be treated as a rule, not least because its enforcement level might need to be adjusted over time.

Appendix H suggests a set of fine-grained enforcement levels suitable for automated real-time activity. Other circumstances can entail different enforcement levels. For example, one of our clients focusing on data quality created a half-dozen shades of 'accept' vs. 'reject' aimed at incoming data from external organizations.

Remember that the enforcement level for any given rule is always completely independent of the logic expressed by that rule. That way, either of them can be changed on its own at any time. This separation supports highly-agile business capabilities.

Question 3:
What Guidance Message?

Violations of rules are always potent teaching moments. There is no better way imaginable to dispense knowledge in real time, especially in automated fashion.

Violations of rules are
potent teaching moments.

Consider the No-Shirt, No-Service Rule. Presumably, the rule is posted visibly at the entrance to the restaurant. When a shirtless person who seeks to dine is turned away, they have been memorably informed of the restaurant's policy.

Of course, such 'education' could prove painful, embarrassing, or even enraging if not softened in some fashion. Preparing the host with some disarming message would probably be prudent – perhaps something like "The owner is pretty old-school. If I let you in without a shirt I could be fired. Just throw on a t-shirt and you'll be fine."

Here's the point. The rule itself always provides the logic behind violations. The No-Shirt, No-Service Rule speaks for itself, just like any other rule should. But sometimes additional messaging is useful or wise. Such messaging can clarify the rule, indicate the rule's motivation, tutor participants, or provide some solution(s). See Chapter III-3 for additional discussion.

Two quick additional points:

- We use the term *guidance message* rather than *violation message* because rules that are guidelines just support guidance, not enforcement.
- Who sees which guidance messages in what context is always a matter of concern. For example, you probably don't want a trespasser to see your what-to-do-in-case-of-trespassing rules when the trespasser causes a violation. Sensitive rules and other guidance messages should be made available only on a selective, need-to-know basis.

Question 4: What Special Violation Response?

Violation of a rule is often an occasion for selective, on-the-spot remediation. Such responses could be aimed at mitigating risks (think computer hack) or seizing opportunities. Consider the No-Shirt, No-Service Rule.

Rejecting a shirtless customer risks displeasing the customer. How could the restaurant soothe ruffled feathers? Perhaps a discount coupon could be offered as an enticement for a future visit. Does the rejected customer seem unruly? Perhaps a message should be sent silently to the manager.

Instead, the occasion might be viewed an opportunity. Perhaps the shirtless customer could be offered a low-cost t-shirt to wear emblazoned with the restaurant's logo, name, etc. The customer's business would be salvaged, plus the restaurant gets free advertising when the t-shirt is worn subsequently.

Violation responses always involve some kind of action, which might or might not be automated. They can generally be any of the following:

- processes or procedures (e.g., to assist in fixing the problem)
- posting of penalties or incentives (e.g., a fine)
- special messages or displays (e.g., an alarm, warning light, etc.)
- scheduling an event (e.g., a review to ensure the problem is resolved)
- enforcement of other rules (See Appendix I for an example involving warranties.)

Aside: The execution of any violation response, as for all actions, takes matters outside the guidance knowledgebase (rulebook). Logically, side effects are unpredictable. Refer to Appendix B.)

A rule can have multiple violation responses, as warranted. The same violation response can also be shared by multiple rules. Since violation responses are not part of a rule per se, they can be changed independently of the rule(s). They are always optional.

At this point you might be wondering about the 'no-service' part of the No-Shirt, No-Service Rule. Doesn't that phrasing suggest an action of some sort (e.g., *deny entrance*)? And you are right to ask! What works as a posted message doesn't always work well as a formal statement of guidance. I'll return to posted messages in Chapter III-3.

Question 5: What Applicability Conditions?

Sometimes different enforcement levels, guidance messages, and/or violation responses apply to the very same base rule in different situations or circumstances. Applicability conditions permit highly-nuanced responses to detected violations – that is, situational sensitivity and situational awareness.

Suppose the restaurant decides to relax enforcement of the No-Shirt, No-Service Rule at certain times. Perhaps the clientele at those times is different, a new business opportunity presents itself, or management wants to take some pressure off staff. For example, management might promote the concept of 'grunge lunches' (lax dress code) on Friday and Saturday.

Specifying applicability conditions for the base No-Shirt, No-Service Rule allows differential enforcement to support 'grunge lunches'.

> Grunge Lunch Applicability Condition: *Lunch time on Friday and Saturday*
>
> > Enforcement Level: *guideline*
>
> Business-As-Usual Applicability Condition: *All other times*
>
> > Enforcement Level: *strictly enforced*

Applicability conditions are subject to certain usage constraints. Refer to Appendix J. Two more ways in which applicability constraints prove quite useful:

- To provide a special way of handling 'exceptions' (exceptional circumstances) for the very same rule. Refer to Chapter IV-1 for discussion and an additional example.
- To reduce the overall number of rules to be captured and managed, thereby to help maintain the focus on core guidance.

This second point is especially important. Consider the following example: Suppose a parking rule has a limit of one hour with a grace period of 10 minutes. At the one-hour mark you get a warning (maybe a flashing red light). If not resolved by the 70-minute mark, you get a citation. Those are not two rules. They're just one, with different applicability conditions.

Also, as this parking example suggests, applicability conditions are an important means to escalate reactions to unresolved violations.

Chapter I-5

About Definitional Rules: What Counts?

Definitional rules literally tell you what counts as an instance of a concept and what doesn't. Examples:

- Does a tank top count as a shirt?
- Does a prospect count as a customer?
- Does a subsidiary's customer count toward a company's market share?

Ever wonder why different people can count the very same things and come up with different answers? Do you suspect key performance indicators (KPIs) you're going by aren't telling exactly the right stories? In referencing or applying a measure, how far might the truth have been stretched?

If you want to count anything precisely, you'll probably need definitional rules in addition to definitions. Come along on this short travel story and let's explore the matter together.

Definitional rules allow you to count things precisely.

Personal Count of Cities-Visited

How many of the following cities have you visited? Count 'em up. I'll tell you my personal count at the end of the chapter.

Abu Dhabi	Casablanca	Lagos	Munich	Shanghai
Amsterdam	Copenhagen	Las Vegas	New Delhi	Singapore
Athens	Dubai	Lisbon	New York	Stockholm
Auckland	Dublin	London	Osaka	Taipei
Bangkok	Glasgow	Los Angeles	Paris	Timbuktu
Barcelona	Hanoi	Manila	Perth	Tokyo
Beijing	Hong Kong	Melbourne	Prague	Toronto
Beirut	Honolulu	Miami	Rio de Janeiro	Vancouver
Berlin	Istanbul	Milan	Rome	Vienna
Budapest	Jakarta	Montreal	Santiago	Warsaw
Cairo	Jerusalem	Moscow	Sao Paolo	Wellington
Cape Town	Kyiv	Mumbai	Seoul	Zurich

The precision of your answer depends entirely on your definitional rules. Here are some questions you might want to ask about your personal city count.

- If you connect flights in an airport but you never physically leave the airport, does that count as a city you've visited? For example, I have connected on same-day flights in and out of Singapore, but as a transient passenger, I could not go outside customs. Does Singapore count for me?
- If you are a passenger in a hired car without input about the route and you pass through a city without stopping or veering from the predetermined route, does that count as a city you have visited? For example, I have passed through Berlin on a chauffeured drive from Amsterdam to Dresden. Does Berlin count? (By the way we were mostly

on the autobahn after midnight, so the trip didn't take as long as you might think!)

- If you were on a cruise ship that had an outbreak of a pandemic and you anchored at a port but could not leave the ship, would that city count? Luckily, I do not have a personal example of this case(!).

By the way, is Singapore a country or a city?! Better check the definitional rules on that!

The Freedom-of-Movement Rule

My daughter and I have had the same kinds of questions in a different travel game. We each keep track of the number of U.S. states and Canadian provinces we have visited. Like daughter, like father, we are both fierce competitors.

So, to resolve edge cases, we had to come up with a what-counts rule to go by. Rules help keep peace in the family(!) – just as for any other group or community of people. By the way, my personal counts for this state-and-province travel game are also at the end of the chapter.

Our solution was what we called the Freedom-of-Movement Rule. To say you have visited a state or province, you must have the opportunity (even if you don't necessarily take it) to move freely about. For the cities-visited game, the Freedom-of-Movement Rule would disallow counting Singapore and Berlin and any city where a quarantined cruise ship might have docked.

My daughter once drove us more than 50 miles out of our way in Minnesota to cross the border into Wisconsin so she could count that state. She just did a U-turn at the first legal opportunity. But Wisconsin counts for her – *freedom of movement!*

Actually, we were over the border for literally only 5-6 minutes. Do you think that's too short a time to count as a visit? What would your rule be for minimum length of visit? Do you think you should at least have to buy something (even if just gasoline)? Money talks of course. Or eat something? Or sleep a night there?

Here's another consideration. My daughter and I have mostly traveled by plane and automobile, seldom by train. Suppose you took a sight-seeing train trip across the continent, you ate and slept on the train, and never stepped off in some states or provinces. Would those count?!

Motivation Matters

The natural tendency in the city/state/province counts is probably to inflate. A higher number looks more impressive. But suppose I told you I was willing to finance your visits to places you've never visited. (By the way, I'm not.) Then you might be a little more conservative in your count. *Motivation matters!*

Or suppose the count is the crime rate in some place. You are a city official responsible for promoting your city to out-of-towners for tours, conventions, and conferences. You'd be tempted to discount the crime rate some, wouldn't you?!

My earlier visit examples and counts are all just games. Counts in business and government, however, are a serious matter. Want to be data-driven? If factual numbers matter to you, you better know the definitional rules!

If you want to be data-driven,
know the definitional rules.

Behavioral Rules and Definitional Rules

Behavioral rules can be specified without definitions and definitional rules, but such behavioral rules almost always prove vague and ineffective.

Consider the (behavioral) No-Shirt, No-Service Rule. For it to be practical, you need a *shirt* definition to start with, then because of all the nuances of *shirt*, probably some (definitional) What's-a-Shirt Rule(s) as well.

Defining terms, and clarifying those definitions with definitional rules, is a fundamental necessity of rules for groups and communities of people. Ever hear of that little thing called 'terms and conditions'?!

My Personal Visit Counts

Here are my personal visit counts as of writing this chapter in January, 2022. They are actually the very same as in January, 2020. I was planning many more visits in the intervening two years, but the pandemic, unfortunately, had other ideas.

My Personal Count of the Cities: 29

My Personal Count of U.S. States and Canadian Provinces: 49 and 10, respectively

You might be curious which state I'm missing. The answer is Alaska, my planned 2020 trip a casualty of the pandemic. By the way, there are 10 provinces in Canada. Many (most?) Canadians have not been to all 10, so I do take a bit of pleasure in that particular count.

Part I Summary

About Rules

A rule is a guide for conduct or action. It provides criteria for judging or evaluating that conduct or action. Every rule tends to remove some degree of freedom. Rules are how you create order from disorder within a community and ensure consistent experience. You'll always resort to explicit rules whenever you want to be able to explain the 'why' of results.

The key feature of rules for groups and communities of people is that individuals and organizations will sometimes break the rules. Instead of dancing all around the fact that rules can be violated, we should entertain it directly. The two fundamental kinds of rules:

- *Behavioral rules* can be violated. They aim to directly shape people's behavior by setting boundaries for acceptable behavior. Some boundaries are meant to be hard ones; other boundaries are meant to be soft ones, as for guidelines. Attempted or actual violations of rules are potent teaching moments providing opportunities to dispense knowledge in real time.
- *Definitional rules* literally tell you what counts as an instance of a concept and what doesn't. They allow you to count things precisely. They provide precision to supplement definitions where misapplying behavioral rules is a significant risk.

In business and government, it is impossible to foresee every circumstance that might occur and for each, prepare in advance, procedural or inference-based scenarios that can execute automatically. Why even try?! Your rules approach needs to be as friendly as possible to real-time insertion of sentiment, human discretion, and common sense. Behavioral rules are the key in that regard.

Wrapped up in rules is important knowledge that can be passed on to others' advantage, not least of which is to avoid risks. If you want to communicate and retain knowledge, rules are key.

Everyone bemoans poor data quality. We fail to understand that rules for business and rules for data are the very *same* rules. To prevent problems with data, rules should be applied in real time wherever possible. If you want to be data-driven, know your rules.

Along with penalties and incentives, policies and rules represent the gear box of governance. If you create policies someone – maybe you, maybe someone else – will need to interpret them. What do you get when you interpret policies? *Rules*.

Part II
Expressing Rules

What makes a good rule statement? Five fundamental criteria for expressing rules are discussed in this Part:

- Being practicable
- Being declarative
- Being factual
- Being complete
- Being unambiguous

Perhaps the most important principle for expressing rules is *no hidden semantics*. You should never have to 'read between the lines' to grasp a rule's meaning. If you want to avoid ambiguity and misinterpretation, every rule should say exactly what it means, and mean exactly what it says.

You should never have to 'read between the lines' to grasp a rule's meaning.

I strongly believe rules in business and government should be *communicated and communal* in the sense that they are not written by a priesthood (software developers, knowledge engineers, or others) who have a lock on reading and interpreting them.

Obviously, only those authorized should see certain rules. Having software knowledge, however, should never be a factor in whether you are authorized.

Chapter II-1

Being Practicable

Suppose you are in training to be a host at a restaurant. You read or hear the following statement.

Customers need to be properly attired.

It's obviously important that you know this. The guidance is basic knowledge for the restaurant's community of people (workers, customers, etc.). It helps set the tone the restaurant wants to maintain.

But are you ready to go to work yet? *No.* "Properly attired" could mean anything from tuxedos and formal gowns, to bathing suits and bathrobes. You almost certainly don't know enough yet. The guidance is not yet ready to put into practice.

Let's be careful here. The guidance is not yet ready to put into practice if you want to be *rule-based* about it. Obviously, any guidance can be arbitrarily enforced (or not). So, let's assume you want to be fair and open about enforcement; in other words, you want a high degree of consistency and impartiality. (In society as a whole, this notion is called *rule of law.*)

What's needed for the guidance then? You need more to go by. The original statement needs to be interpreted into a more specific form. Perhaps that's how we arrived at the No-Shirt, No-Service Rule in Chapter I-3. Much more concrete. Yet we found even that rule might not be sufficient for being rule-based in the sense we mean. So, then we arrived at some What's-a-Shirt Rule(s).

And there are other questions you should ask. Is the intent of the rule to disallow service, but not entry? Perhaps the true intent is *no-shirt-no-entry.*

This drill-down from high-level guidance to rules specific enough to be put into practice is a central requirement of rules for groups and communities of people. Retaining memory of these drill-downs (traceability) is, in turn, a key area that platforms should support. (Refer to the Conclusion of this book.)

Drill-down from high-level guidance to rules specific enough to be put into practice is a central requirement of rules for groups and communities of people.

Another Example

Suppose someone in authority states:

Safety is our first concern.

They've obviously said something quite important. It doesn't really matter whether they call it a policy, principle, doctrine, goal, or whatever. It provides high-level guidance and helps establish priorities. It's a key bit of knowledge.

But does the statement tell you exactly what behavior is expected? *No*. It gives no specific criteria to go by – nothing to judge whether or not you are in compliance. What exactly counts? Any evaluation will be highly subjective – not rule-based in a meaningful way.

Now suppose someone in authority says:

A hard hat must be worn in a construction site.

Suppose they also give you adequate definitions and/or definitional rules for 'hard hat' and 'construction site'. Now could you act as an impartial judge in determining whether or not a particular worker is in compliance? You're certainly much closer now because you have an explicit criterion to judge by.

But wait. Did you notice that the statement does not say the hard hat must be worn *on a person's head?* Would it be acceptable to 'wear' the hard hat somehow buckled to the worker's belt? Actually, the rule currently doesn't even mention *person* or *head*. Are we to punish hard hats themselves for lying around not being worn?! Policy interpreters and rule analysts need to be careful readers, as well as highly imaginative in playing out different scenarios.

Policy interpreters and rule analysts need to be careful readers, as well as highly imaginative in playing out different scenarios.

Am I being too picky? If you're a person in a construction site, and a brick happens to fall on your head, *probably not(!)*. And if you're the company facing giant liability suits, probably not either. Here's a more complete version:

Revised Hard Hat Rule: *Every person must wear a hard hat on their head while in a construction site.*

There are always substantial risks in groups and communities of people. These risks often merit a high degree of completeness in expressing relevant rules. Being complete in expressing rules is discussed more in Chapter II-4.

The Gold Standard for Expressing Rules

There is no way to be rule-based about compliance, determinations, and counts unless rules are specific and definitive. Good rules avoid subjectivity and the impossible. They have been interpreted (drilled down) to a point that they can be used or applied directly. In other words, good rules are ready to put into practice. They are *practicable*.

Good rules have been interpreted (drilled down) to a point that they are ready to put into practice. They are practicable.

Aside: If discretion is warranted in applying a rule, it should be exercised in full knowledge of the context and circumstances for which the rule was intended.

Here's the test for whether a rule is practicable:

A rule is practicable if any person who knows about the rule can observe a relevant situation (including his or her own behavior) and determine directly whether or not the rule is being complied with.

One important caveat: The person either needs to know the business vocabulary or have access to it (including all relevant definitional rules). Assuming that's the case, the person should be able to read any practicable statement and be able to fully understand it without external clarification. Creating practicable statements is a must wherever you can't depend on conversation for explanation – in other words, it's a must for all formal communication.

By the way, just because a statement sounds authoritative doesn't mean it's practicable. Consider the following example from one of our clients:

Statement: *The product type, vaccine type, and manufacturer for vaccine dose must not be contradictory.*

Sure. But what are the criteria to determine whether or not the product type, vaccine type, and manufacturer are contradictory for a vaccine dose?! The statement is obviously important, but it is merely a policy or a principle, not a practicable rule. Don't be fooled!

Achieving practicable rules in effect means squeezing out *wiggle room*. The 'squeezing' can be no small chore for policy interpreters and professional analysts.

Achieving practicable rules means squeezing out wiggle room.

Here's a possibly disturbing thought for you. Many software developers know far less about specific areas of regulation, business knowledge, and organizational priorities than policy makers and subject matter experts. Do you really want software developers making assumptions about the intent of 'un-squeezed' rules?!

No, better to have people in the know do that. Don't abdicate responsibility!

Wiggle Room and Automation

Squeezing out the wiggle room from rules is necessary no matter whether you automate a rule or not. In fact, it might be even more important if the rule is automated. Humans can apply common sense. Computers (as yet) cannot.

But that's not the end of the story with respect to automation and behavioral rules, in at least two respects.

- First, rule platforms absolutely need to be more accepting of natural language in expressing rules, if for no other reason than better governance. (See the book's Conclusion.)
- Second, AI and machine learning (ML) are rapidly changing the game with respect to detecting violations. Let me give you an example.

For many years I used the hard-hat rule as an example of a rule that *couldn't* be automated. Then some years ago I started learning about automated facial recognition. I thought to myself,

"Hmm, if a machine can recognize a face, surely it ought to be able to recognize whether or not someone is wearing a hard hat (on their head)."

I hope I learned my lesson. These days you can *never* be too sure about whether behavioral rules can be automated(!).

> *Aside:* Practicable definitional rules are always automatable. If any relevant facts are missing, however, they sometimes cannot be evaluated.

For better or for worse, we're sure to see significant and ever-expanding opportunities to use bots in supporting behavioral rules.

We'll see significant and ever-expanding opportunities to use bots in supporting behavioral rules.

Chapter II-2

Being Declarative

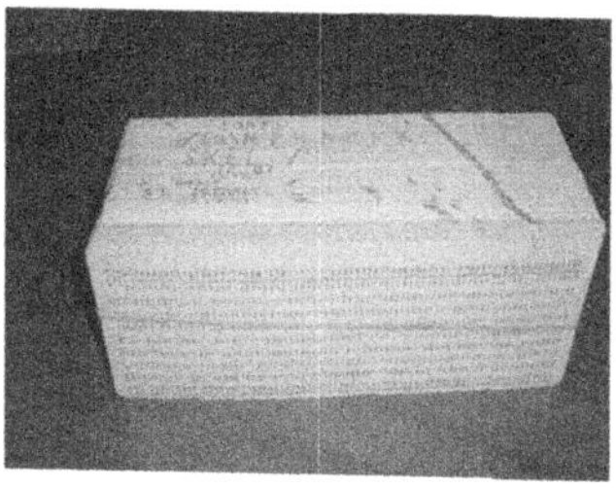

The picture at right still makes me a bit queasy. The single rubber band to hold the deck of punch cards together just looks too flimsy to me.

You see I went to graduate school for computer science classes in the early 1970s.

Aside: If you the reader are younger than 60 and not interested in history, go to "Thought Experiment for Procedural vs. Declarative Specifications" below. (Ah, a notorious 'go to' instruction!)

The Deck History

In those days we used punch cards to specify and execute computer programs. Keeping a deck of punch cards in the right order was a huge 'programming' concern. Drop them on the floor accidentally and you risked spending the entire evening in the computer lab (which happened often anyway, given the slow turn-around of operations).

Those were the days of mainframe computers. Virtually all software development was done in-house, in batch. Jobs were submitted as decks of cards (sometimes quite large) and came back as paper printouts (several hours or even a day later). Often, a job had to be re-run many times to get it right. The outputs took the form of over-sized, folded listings, sometimes inches thick. Those were the days. *Not!*

So, you went to the lab armed with boxes of the strongest rubber bands you could find and magic markers of different colors to draw diagonal lines across the outer edges of decks. Every student had lived the nightmare of dropping decks, so the following thought experiment really hit home.

Thought Experiment for Procedural vs. Declarative Specifications

I suppose this thought experiment has lost some of its punch over the years (pun intended) since we no longer use physical media to specify programming logic. But you'll get the point anyway. It's still the best analogy I've ever heard to explain the difference between declarative specifications vs. procedural specifications.

Here are the instructions:

1. Write a computer program.
2. Specify each statement on a separate card.
3. Give the deck of cards to operations to execute.
4. Make sure the program runs properly and has no bugs.
5. Take the rubber band(s) off the deck and throw the cards high up in the air.
6. Pick the cards up in random order off the floor (making sure you haven't lost any and they are all right-side up).
7. Give the deck to operations to execute again.
8. Inspect the results. If the logic still executes properly, it's declarative. If not, it's procedural.

So simple, yet so powerful a test! Here's what it means:

- If the program still works properly, there are *no hidden semantics* in the logic. The order of presentation of the cards (statements) to the machine for execution makes no difference to the outcome.
- If the program *doesn't* still work properly, then not all the semantics could be accessed by the machine even after

reading the entire deck. Some were hidden 'in-between' the individual cards; that is, implicit in the sequence of instructions.

Aside: Don't mistake logical dependence for sequential dependence. For example, if the calculation of net profit depends on the calculation of gross income, obviously gross income has to be calculated first, even if not the first statement presented. But a machine can figure that out, just like a human can, based on the term 'gross income' common to both rules.

In rules for business and government, *hidden semantics* in rules is never good. Communities of people and organizations must share understanding of rules, and they can't do that if meaning is withheld. So, rules for business and government should always be purely declarative. Sequence should never matter!

Rules for business and government should always be purely declarative. Sequence should never matter.

Separation of Concerns

Let's be very clear here about what I'm saying and what I'm *not* saying. I'm *not* saying that instructions and procedures (sequenced sets of instructions) are a bad thing. It goes without saying they're extremely important. How could we live without them!

For example, the only way I could have communicated the thought experiment above effectively was as a procedure. I couldn't have expressed it as rules. And why would I even want to try?! In no way, shape, or form do rules substitute for procedures or processes. Rules simply tell you what results are correct.

Look at it this way. Without actions, procedures, and processes, the state of the world would never change. We obviously don't live in a static world, and couldn't even if we wanted to. Actions, procedures, and processes (transforms) are a fundamental fact of life.

Rules for communities and groups of people serve a different purpose. They never make things happen; they simply express which states of affairs are allowed (desirable) or more importantly, which are *not* allowed (undesirable). Rules are *imposed* on actions.

As a consequence, you never want to mix or confuse rules and instructions. You always want to be clear which is which. By 'mix', I specifically mean two things:

- A 'rule' should never call for the execution of an action. If it does, it's not a true rule; it's an instruction and should be treated as such. (Notorious in this regard are 'rules' calling on the infamous CRUD words – *create, retrieve, update, delete.* These are pure (data) system actions.)
- Even if an individual rule is expressed declaratively, it should never be included as a step in a procedure (set of instructions). Implicitly, including an individual rule at a certain place in a sequenced set of instructions turns the rule into an instruction.

A rule should never call for the execution of an action.

Keeping the distinction between rules (declarative) and instructions (procedural) is an important task for policy interpreters and analysts. Subject matter experts often want to tell you *how* to do things, so their tendency is to talk procedurally.

How is important, of course. Equally important for groups and communities of people, however, is expressing criteria (rules) for the correctness of what happens. Keep them distinct! Instructions are about the right things to do to get something done; rules are about getting things right no matter how they are done.

Instructions are about doing the right things; rules are about doing things right.

Conditional Instructions

Let's look at some additional examples. Chapter I-2 included the following:

> Sign Posted on Glass Box Containing an Ax: *In case of fire, break glass.*

This statement is conditional ("in case of fire") but gives an instruction ("break glass"). It calls for the execution of an action. It is not a rule. For the same reason, all the following are conditional instructions, not rules:

- If the plastic tears, fix it with duct tape.
- If the game is important to you, jump on the first plane to get there.
- Before the grenade is thrown, remove the safety pin.

A distinctive feature of all instructions, whether conditional or not, is that it makes a difference what order they are evaluated in. Let's suppose instead of just one sign, you see two signs posted near each other:

> Sign Posted on Glass Box Containing an Ax: *In case of fire, break glass.*

> Sign Posted near Elevators: *In case of fire, exit building using stairs.*

Which instruction you act on first makes a big difference. If you perform former first, you will probably exit the building with broken glass on the floor and perhaps an ax in your hand. If you perform the latter instruction first, the glass will likely remain unbroken and the ax where it is. Those states of the world are very different.

Rules should never work that way. Since rules perform no actions, it makes no difference whatsoever what order you (or a machine) read them in. They all apply equally. Collectively, they simply tell you whether the state of the world in between actions is correct – that is, allowed (desirable) or not allowed (undesirable). No small matter! For more about the importance of the distinction between rules and actions, refer to Appendix B.

Rules tell you whether the state of the world in between actions is correct

Again, let's be very clear here what I'm saying and what I'm *not* saying. I'm *not* saying that instructions are a bad thing. It goes without saying they're extremely important. A world without instructions would be plenty confusing! Indeed, as discussed in Chapter III-3, instructions can play a very important role alongside rules in messaging. But before we get there, some other important matters need to be discussed first.

Chapter II-3

Being Factual

As discussed in previous chapters, none of the following are appropriate in expressing rules:

- Instructions
- Commands (conditional or otherwise)
- Processes, procedures, and actions

What's left then as proper form for expressing rules? *Facts*, or more precisely, *factual expressions*.

When I say 'facts' it might or might not occur to you to think 'data'. But you should. They're intimately connected. A great many problems involving both ambiguity and data quality arise from lack of awareness about this connection. Refer to Appendix L.

About Facts

When I say 'fact' you should think of a sentence taken to be true. Suppose I state:

The Eiffel Tower is located in Paris.

That's a fact. I've personally verified it to be true. I have seen the Eiffel Tower with my own eyes, touched it, and ridden the elevator to the top. Facts are a basic element of knowledge.

> *Aside:* Actually, rather than 'sentence' I should say 'proposition' because the same proposition can be expressed in many ways and in different natural languages.

Obviously not every sentence is true. Suppose I said, "Mt. Fuji is in New Zealand." That's verifiably not true.

So generally, to be a fact a sentence needs to be stipulated as such.

- In law, facts are included in fact patterns decided by a judge or jury.
- In journalism, facts are established by corroboration.
- In IT business systems, facts are generally indicated by the presence of data in databases.
- For business knowledge, facts are structured using a concept model.[6]

Rules vs. Facts

Rules go a step farther than facts. A rule prescribes something about some factual expression *always* or *never* being true. A rule is not an actual fact about the world per se but rather about the world as a group or community of people would have it be.

A rule prescribes something about some factual expression always or never being true.

Suppose you say in your business "Our customers have names." Or you might say "Some customers have names." You might even say, "As of this moment, every one of our customers has a name." Let's assume each statement is true – that is, all are facts.

Still, tomorrow a customer might come along that doesn't have a name. What you have not yet said explicitly is that you want to avoid any nameless customers. For that you need to express a rule, perhaps:

Rule: *Every customer has a name.*

6 Refer to: *Business Knowledge Blueprints: Enabling Your Data to Speak the Language of the Business* (2nd ed), by Ronald G. Ross, 2020.

For some factual expression to express a rule, you must communicate your special intent about that expression always or never being true. In other words, you must somehow explicitly indicate the intended 'ruleness' of the expression.

There are many ways to indicate this 'ruleness'. In the example above, the text is literally prefixed by 'Rule'. That was no accident. Or, you might have used a keyword such as 'must' in a context where it is clear you are writing rules.[7]

Every customer must have a name.

No matter what method is used, to represent a rule a factual expression must somehow be 'stamped' as such if that is what is intended. Left implicit, you can never be sure.

A factual expression must be 'stamped' as a rule if that is what is intended.

Inserting factual expressions into decision tables also 'stamps' them as rules. (See Appendix C.) Unfortunately, a significant majority of rules don't fit into decision tables. So, other forms of 'stamping' ruleness is required. *Bad* ways to 'stamp' ruleness include:

- Depending on IF-THEN syntax. (Refer to Appendix K.)
- Using a proprietary language or interface, which risks platform lock-in.

Aside: Interoperability for textual business statements (not just rules) is a central goal of the OMG specification SBVR.

---

[7] Refer to www.RuleSpeak.com, currently available in seven languages, for guidelines to write rules in structured natural language. In RuleSpeak® for English, the keywords for 'stamping' sentences as behavioral rules are *must* and *only*. RuleSpeak was one of three reference languages used by OMG specification SBVR *(Semantics of Business Vocabulary and Business Rules)*, which does not standardize any particular language for rules.

Let's take another example. Suppose I assert the following is true:

A customer is charged a fee for a bank wire.

Fact or rule? As the text stands, it's impossible to tell. Since a rule is different than everyday facts, assuming 'fact' is probably safest. To indicate 'rule', you need something extra. You must 'stamp' the text as a rule. For example, you can do one or both of the following:

- 'Stamp' the sentence internally using a keyword such as 'must'.

  A customer must be charged a fee for a bank wire.

- 'Stamp' the sentence externally using a suitable prefix or other device.

  Rule: *A customer is charged a fee for a bank wire.*

Aside: Formally, indicating a factual expression as definitively expressing a rule (or other form of guidance) requires an indication of modality. Refer to Appendix F. This indication can also be achieved by keyword (e.g., 'must' for obligation) or an appropriate context of authoring.

Most rules are more complex with regard to facts. Example:

Agent Rule: *A customer must be assigned to an agent if the customer has placed an order.*

This rule uses a two-part factual expression:

Part 1: *a customer is assigned to an agent*
Part 2: *the customer has placed an order*

Rules, Facts, and Concepts

A more complex rule can involve a significant number of parts or conditions, sometimes a dozen or more. But each rule isn't based on its own unique set of concepts; the same underlying concepts are used over and over again in different rules. (In other words, the relationship between rules and the concepts underlying them is many-to-many.)

So, a blueprint for expressing the rules is quite helpful. Here is a partial concept model diagram supporting the rule above.

Figure 1. *Partial Concept Model Diagram Supporting the Agent Rule*

A concept model diagram does not show actual facts or rules; instead, it shows the concepts needed to express those facts and rules consistently, specifically:

- noun concepts, as indicated using boxes labeled by terms.
- verb concepts, as indicated using worded lines and arrows.

More examples are presented in later chapters. Not incidentally, each term in a concept model diagram requires a solid business definition. A box on a diagram – even a labeled box – means nothing without adequate definitional criteria (business definition and/or definitional rules).

Expressing Rules

In a given natural language, there is no single correct way to express the same rule. There are good ways and bad ways, of course, but even following all dictates of grammar and of ruleness as outlined in these chapters, it's still possible to have alternative versions. For example, both the following rules mean the same:

Rule 1: *The sum total of an order must not exceed $10,000.*

Rule 2: *The total amount of an order must not be greater than $10,000.*

If that happens, pick the version that best communicates the meaning, or keep both as synonymous forms.

One more important point: A rule and the rule statement(s) that express it are not actually the same thing. The easiest way to understand why is to think about multi-language support. In Switzerland, for example, you might have four statements of the same rule, one each in French, German, Italian, and Romansh. The rule is actually the *meaning*, not the statement. (The same is true for facts vs. statements of facts.)

For more about forms of expression for rules refer to Appendix M.

Key Points

Let's condense and summarize the key points in this chapter about being factual in expressing rules:

- Creating rules always involves factual expressions.
- A rule is not an actual fact about the world per se but rather about the world as the community would have it be.

Aside: This statement is true for definitional rules as well as behavioral rules. A definitional rule expressing that all shirts have sleeves is not the same as a fact about any particular shirt. For example, maybe you have simply never come across a shirt before, so you have no shirt-specific facts yet. (Think 'black swan'.)

- By expressing criteria for the desired world, a rule works to constrain facts about that world – and any and all actions seeking to create those facts.
- The 'ruleness' of some factual expression never happens by accident; it must be 'stamped' onto the expression.
- Many rules involve multiple parts or conditions.
- Many different rules are based on the very same concepts.

Chapter II-4

Being Complete

Being complete about expressing a rule means leaving no stones unturned in communicating its full meaning. Let's look at several 'stones' you might stumble over in that regard.

Context

Suppose you are in an airport, about to pass through security. You see a posted sign that says:

Sign Posted at Entrance to Airport Security: *No Photography*

The sign clearly doesn't mean no photography anywhere in the universe. It means no photography in airport security. How do we know? Context provides the clues. We happen to be standing right at that entrance.

Then we proceed into security and we see a sign that says:

Sign in Security: *Jokes will be taken seriously.*

Seriously?! Joking is now literally banned in the whole universe? How sad! No, we are in the context of security. They just mean *there.*

Suppose we are in a video conference. The moderator says:

Video Conference Rule: *All participants should be muted while not speaking.*

Wait! I don't actually have a mute button on my person. So, they must mean the mute button on the device I'm using for the video conference. *Context.* (Personally, I have more trouble remembering to hit *unmute* before talking.)

Suppose you're on a bus and see a sign that says:

Sign on Bus: *No Standing*

No standing anywhere in the universe? No, just while on the bus and the bus is moving. *Context.*

The luxury of communicating within the context of location or conversation is that we can create shorter messages and still convey sufficient meaning for a reasonable person. In writing rules, however, we generally don't have that luxury. So, the relevant context needs to be spelled out in the rules. For example, we can't just write:

Driver Rule: *No driving without a license.*

How about a fishing license? Would that do? Am I allowed to drive golf balls at the practice range? So, instead we must write:

Revised Driver Rule: *Any person operating a motor vehicle on a public roadway must hold a valid driver's license.*

The relevant context needs to be spelled out in writing rules.

Eliminating assumed context is one of the differences between informal communication and formal communication.[8] These differences are well documented by authorities in the field of writing.[9] They actually apply to any kind of formal communication conveying knowledge, not just rules.

Here's another sin of context. In everyday (informal) communication between people, words like 'here', 'now', 'me', 'you', etc. are often taken for granted. Such references are generally easily resolved.

8 Refer to *Business Knowledge Messaging: How to Avoid Business Miscommunication,* by Ronald G. Ross, 2022.

9 *How Languages Work,* by David Crystal, The Overlook Press, Peter Mayer Publishers, Inc., 2005, p. 465

But in writing formal communication, you can never be completely sure who the readers will be, what they know or don't know, and what purpose they may have in reading the material. So, what you write needs to be complete, making no assumptions about context.

Modifiers and Qualifications

Chapter I-3 presented specifications about whether a customer counts (qualifies) as a gold customer. Here's where we left those specifications:

> Definition of Gold Customer: *a customer that regularly places large orders and merits highest-level service*

> Gold Customer Rule: *A customer is considered a gold customer if the customer places more than 12 large orders during a calendar year that are each fully paid within 60 days.*

Did you catch there's no clarification of the modifier 'large' in either the definition or the rule above? Currently the question of large-ness (how large is large?) remains a gap in the business logic. Does it need to be closed? If consistent behavior is important, *yes.*

There are at least three possibilities in this regard, as follows. Your drill-down of the logic is not complete until one of these options (or some other) is selected.

1. Existing facts (stored data) already indicate whether an order is large (yes/no).
2. Facts are requested in an interactive dialog with some user(s) during the rule's evaluation.
3. More rules are written providing criteria for what is meant by 'large'.

In the third case, some additional definitional rule(s) need to be specified, for example:

Large Order Rule: *An order is considered a large order if the order nets more than $999.*

In rules for business and government, the devil often lies in definitional detail. We call pursuit of that detail "pulling the threads." It's an orderly, gap-closing march toward completeness that requires knowing what questions to ask and how to ask them.

In rules for business and government, the devil often lies in definitional detail.

Note that the Large Order Rule actually adds a new term to your business vocabulary, 'large order'. You can use that term in any other rule (in addition to the Gold Customer Rule) without having to respecify the logic. This is an important means by which consistency is achieved across a set of rules.

If you are a close reader, you'll find another gap in the current version of the Gold Customer Rule: What does the qualification "within 60 days" mean? When does the clock start ticking?

- When the order is received?
- When the goods are shipped?
- When the goods arrive?

And when does the clock *stop* ticking?

- When payment is received?
- When the payment is confirmed by the bank?

Qualifications concerning timing like this are quite common in rules. Their logic is not complete until you have explicit criteria for them.

Back to Definitions vs. Definitional Rules

The original definition of 'gold customer' was:

Definition of Gold Customer: *a customer that regularly places large orders and merits highest-level service*

You can easily imagine how dense this definition could become if additional logic from the definitional rules discussed above were loaded into it. Machines could probably handle the density; people, not so much. Keep definitions friendly for people by expressing supplemental definitional rules.

Keep definitions friendly for people by expressing supplemental definitional rules.

Aside: Definitional rules are especially useful where a concept is inherently so mathematical that for practical purposes a definition adds little (e.g., 'average monthly sales'). Consider the concept 'large order'? Does it need an explicit definition in addition to the Large Order Rule? Maybe not. Perhaps that definitional rule is sufficiently clear and complete on its own already.

You might sense I'm saying that definitions should be aimed at basic human communication, whereas definitional rules provide the precision and completeness that machines need. That's only half true – but not the part you might guess. To apply rules consistently, *people* need precision and completeness too.

Chapter II-5

Being Unambiguous

By 'being unambiguous' let me be sure you know exactly what I mean. I do *not* mean being unambiguous beyond all doubt in every aspect of natural language. You'd be surprised how often people think that's what I mean when I talk about eliminating ambiguity. *No!* I stipulate up-front that's impossible (and probably not even desirable).

So, let me be very clear then about the context of this discussion.

- First, I am talking only about rules and other forms of guidance for business and government.
- Second, I assume a structured business vocabulary, such as one based on a concept model. Without a blueprint to go by, all bets are off.
- Third, I assume a writer-and-reader-friendly solution to the pesky problem of ANDs and ORs having no precedence in natural language.[10]

Given these basic caveats, by 'being unambiguous' I mean removing ambiguity *beyond a reasonable doubt* in formal communication.

Here is a simple example of the kind of ambiguity that policy interpreters, business analysts, and IT professionals deal with daily. It's a sentence from the California 2014 Paid Sick Leave Policy.[11]

---

[10] Does 'A and B or C' mean '(A and B) or C,' or 'A and (B or C)'? The problem has a perfectly workable solution. See *Tabulation of Lists in RuleSpeak®: Using "The Following" Clause*, https://www.rulespeak.com/en/RuleSpeak%20Tabulation%20Primer.pdf

[11] https://www.dir.ca.gov/dlse/publications/paid_sick_days_poster_template_(11_2014).pdf

Accrued paid sick leave shall carry over to the following year of employment and may be capped at 48 hours or 6 days.

Ambiguities:

- What is being capped? Is it the amount of accrued paid sick leave in a given period or the amount of sick leave that may be carried forward?
- What is meant by "may be"? ... *Must be?* ... *Can be but need not be?*

These ambiguities must be wrung out of the statement to get a clear interpretation (i.e., unambiguous beyond a reasonable doubt).

As illustrated above, the key to disambiguation is forming the right questions to ask. A good reader of formal messages 'sees' the questions that should be asked. A good writer of formal messages avoids them in the first place.

Key to disambiguation is forming the right questions to ask.

Disambiguation is a fundamental skill for policy interpreters and professional analysts – indeed, for any writer of formal communications. This chapter illustrates disambiguation using two typical examples.

Example 1

Consider this statement:

An order must not be shipped if the outstanding balance exceeds credit authorization.

On a quick first reading this statement might seem clear enough. Look closer, however, and the meaning becomes murky. Important clarifications are missing or hidden from view.

- Outstanding balance *of what?* The *what* might be *order, customer, account, shipment* – or something else altogether.
- Credit authorization *of what?* Again, the *what* might be *order, customer, account, shipment* – or something else.

To disambiguate the statement, suppose you pursue these questions and discover that:

- account *has* outstanding balance
- account *is held by* customer
- customer *places* order
- customer *has* credit authorization

How do you find these things out? Hopefully, your concept model informs you. No concept model? You need a blueprint, so time to start building one now.[12] You're likely to come across the same ambiguities time and time again. Refer to Appendix E for a brief discussion of concept models.

Using the clarifications, the ambiguities in the statement can be eliminated. The result is the following (new portions underlined based on the discoveries above):[13]

An order must not be shipped if the outstanding balance of the account held by the customer that places the order exceeds the credit authorization of the customer.

The statement has now been disambiguated *beyond a reasonable doubt.* Of course, that assumes the meanings of the terms it includes are agreed, but that's another purpose of creating a concept model. The statement now makes *deep sense,* sufficient for formal messaging. In other words, it is practicable, as discussed in Chapter II-1.

[12] Refer to *Business Knowledge Blueprints: Enabling Your Data to Speak the Language of the Business* (2nd ed), by Ronald G. Ross, 2020.

[13] We use the RuleSpeak® guidelines to express rules: www.RuleSpeak.com. Think of RuleSpeak as an interpretation disambiguator. It supports building a common communication community among business people, business analysts, and IT professionals for textual rules.

Example 1 highlights some very important points about rule analysis.

- The central activity is *interpretation*. You take statements that are less than fully clear and interpret them into statements that are more fully clear. A key skill for this kind of interpretation is the ability to disambiguate.
- Interpretation happens just about everywhere in business and government. It is a key component of how business capabilities are operationalized.
- Recording acts of interpretation (who interpreted what, when, in what ways, and for what reasons) is central to traceability, good business governance, and corporate memory.[14] For more, refer to the Conclusion of this book.

Recording acts of interpretation is central to traceability, good business governance, and corporate memory.

Example 2

This second example is a bit more complicated. It's from a client in the mortgage industry.

> *Income must be greater than 20% of the estimated value if subject to litigation.*

Questions that arise in interpreting this sentence include:

- Income of *what*?
- Estimated value of *what*?
- *What* is subject to litigation?

Since the subject matter pertains to loan applications, it's a safe bet that the sentence pertains to *property*. Unfortunately, as

[14] Refer to *Business Knowledge Messaging: How to Avoid Business Miscommunication*, by Ronald G. Ross, 2022, Chapter 9.

happens so often in informal messaging, that context has been assumed in the sentence. So, if that's correct, *property* should be referenced explicitly.

How things are related in mortgage knowledge is complex, so at this point we won't make much progress without a blueprint to go by. Figure 1 presents a partial concept model diagram to help out. Lines in the diagram have been numbered to assist in the subsequent discussion.

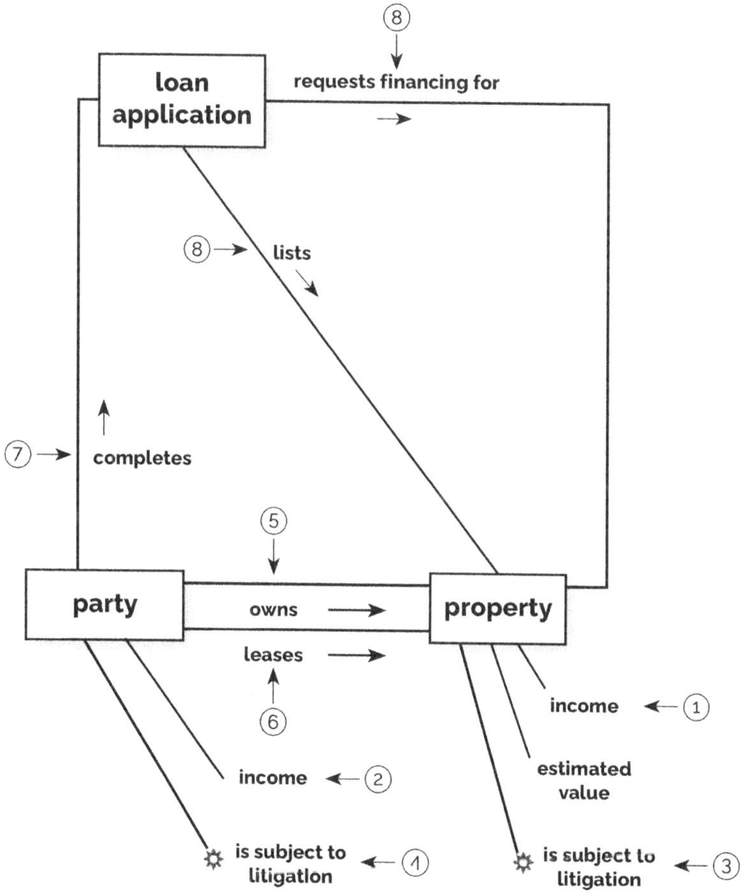

Figure 1. *Concept Model Diagram Supporting Loan Applications*

Here's a quick explanation of the notation.[15]

- Boxes labeled by appropriate terms represent noun concepts.
- Lines represent verb concepts (so facts and rules can be expressed).
- Arrows beside lines between boxes indicate which direction to 'read' the wordings for verb concepts.
- Lines without explicit wordings to unboxed terms default to the wording 'has'.
- Lines with sunburst symbols at one end represent unary verb concepts (which evaluate only to true, false, or unknown for any given party or property).

Now let's focus on disambiguating the original sentence. We can see from the diagram that *estimated value* pertains to *property*. That much is clear. But several ambiguities are now apparent for the sentence:

- *Income* could pertain either to property (1) or to party (2).
- *Property* is subject to litigation (3), but so is party (4).

Disambiguation requires resolving these ambiguities – in other words, clarifying *which* income the sentence refers to and *what* is subject to litigation.

Let's focus on the former ambiguity first. Which income is being talked about? And in what way does *income* relate to *property*? Review of the diagram reveals more potential resolutions than you might imagine – at least five. These resolutions are expressed below using relevant wordings for the respective verb concepts:

1. The income (1) *is of* the property.
2. The income (2) *is of* the party who *owns* (5) the property.
3. The income (2) *is of* the party who *leases* (6) the property.

[15] For detailed explanation of the notation refer to *Business Knowledge Blueprints: Enabling Your Data to Speak the Language of the Business* (2nd ed), by Ronald G. Ross, 2020.

4. The income (2) *is of* the party who *completes* (7) a loan application that lists (8) the property (as collateral).
5. The income (2) *is of* the party who *completes* (7) a loan application *requesting financing for* (8) the property.

Picking the right answer is a matter of knowing the business knowledge. Subject matter experts will tell you that resolution 5 is the correct interpretation. They also will clarify that the sentence pertains to *property* being subject to litigation, not *party*.

Now wordings for the relevant verb concepts can be worked into the sentence to remove ambiguity beyond a reasonable doubt (wordings underlined):

> *The <u>income</u> (2) <u>of the party</u> who <u>completes</u> (7) <u>a loan application requesting financing for</u> (8) <u>a property</u> must be greater than 20% of the estimated value <u>of the property</u> if the <u>property is subject to litigation</u> (3).*

Assuming the terms are properly defined, the rule is now practicable – complete and ready for prime time.

Part II Summary

Expressing Rules

To be rule-based requires rules to be specific and definitive. Good rules avoid subjectivity. They have been interpreted to a point that they can be used or applied directly. In other words, they are ready to put into practice – that is, *practicable*.

A rule is practicable if any person who knows about the rule can observe a relevant situation (including his or her own behavior) and determine directly whether or not the rule is being complied with. Obviously, the person either needs to know the business vocabulary or have access to it.

Rules for business and government should be purely declarative. Their sequence should never matter, nor should a rule ever call for execution of an action. Rules simply tell you whether the state of the world in between actions is correct.

Rules should always be expressed factually. Rules often involve multiple parts or conditions, but many different rules are based on the very same concepts.

A rule is not an actual fact about the world per se, but rather about the world as the group or community of people would have it be. By expressing criteria for the desired world, a rule works to constrain facts about that world – and any and all actions seeking to create those facts. The 'ruleness' of some factual expression never happens by accident; it must be 'stamped' onto the expression.

For rules to be effective, relevant context needs to be spelled out. The devil often lies in the definitional detail. You can keep definitions friendly for people by expressing supplemental definitional rules.

Disambiguation is a fundamental skill for policy interpreters and professional analysts. Key to disambiguation is forming the right questions to ask. Also central is a structured business vocabulary based on a concept model.

Part III

Analyzing Rules

With rules, you're always on a journey of discovery. The challenge (and the fun) for policy interpreters and analysts is knowing the right questions to ask. In the process, you will probe into the very heart of business knowledge, its support, and its communication. We call it "pulling the threads."

With rules, you're always on a journey of discovery.

Your journey of discovery will take you through the following areas:

- Policies, regulations, contractual obligations, and other artifacts pertaining to governance or business knowledge. *What are all the rules? How do you go about interpreting them correctly?*
- Flash Points. *When do rules need to be evaluated? How can you ensure comprehensive evaluation, allowing no events to fall between the cracks?*
- Messaging. *How can you best seize on the messaging opportunities afforded by rules to shape behavior? How do you disseminate business knowledge in real time to those with a need to know?*

This Part of the book addresses these three topics in-depth. The discussion will leave you well-equipped for your journey of discovery into the forest that is business guidance.

Chapter III-1

Discovery of Rules

What skills do you need to analyze formal communications to produce practicable rules in business and government? What does interpretation of source materials require?

This chapter identifies five basic skills you need. To illustrate these skills, it examines the following short bit of text from the policy manual of one of our clients whose mission is to pay claims for health care.

> Cost Share Policy: *The Health Program has a cost share policy. Clients are responsible for the payment of 25% of the cost of the benefit(s) to a maximum contribution of $500 per family per benefit year.*

Like the majority of policies, the text seems deceptively simple and clear at first reading. Poke around a bit though, and questions quickly arise. The guidance is not yet in practicable form – not ready for deployment and implementation.

By no means is this assessment intended as a criticism of the policy. Creating sound policies, aligned with goals and strategy, is hard. Gaps and open issues are inevitable. It's simply our job to sort them out into practicable rules.

Gaps and open issues in policies are inevitable. Our job is to sort them out.

Skill 1. Developing Business Vocabulary

Ignore business vocabulary at your peril. Unaligned assumptions about the meaning of terms, and how they fit together, are perhaps the greatest source of misinterpretation and eventual rework in rule analysis.

Ignore business vocabulary at your peril.

Here are three quick examples for the Cost Share Policy:

1. *Where is 'claim'?* The organization's mission is focused on evaluating and paying (or denying) claims, yet the term is not mentioned at all in the text. Why? When the authors wrote the policy, they probably simply assumed the context 'claims'. The omission, however, leaves a big hole in the meaning.
2. *Who is the 'client'?* Apparently, claims are for health services performed for a patient. Is that correct? If so, is the client the same as the patient? Or someone else in the patient's family? Or someone else altogether? In what ways are people involved in the health-care activities?
3. *What is a 'family'?* Who counts as a member of a family? You need to know in order to determine whether a claim 'counts' toward a family's cost-share responsibility. Hopefully, there are family facts (existing data) to go by. If not, capturing the rules for family membership can prove a particularly thorny area.

So, you need a structured business vocabulary to go by, with standard terms and definitions, based on a concept model.[16] It can be developed in parallel, and iteratively, along with interpretation and development of rules. Refer to Appendix E for a brief discussion of concept models.

Below is the concept model diagram needed for analysis of the Cost-Share Policy. It's partial, but let's assume it's correct as far as it goes. Now you have a blueprint to navigate the concepts and to shape what you write. In the diagram:

- noun concepts are indicated using boxes labeled by terms.
- verb concepts are indicated using worded lines and arrows.
- roles of noun concepts within verb concepts are indicated in brackets.

16 Refer to *Business Knowledge Blueprints: Enabling Your Data to Speak the Language of the Business* (2nd ed), by Ronald G. Ross, 2020.

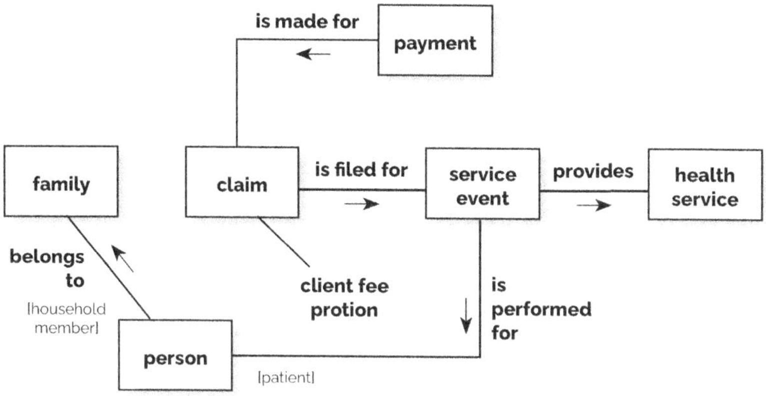

Figure 1. *Concept Model Diagram Supporting the Cost-Share Policy*

Skill 2. Capturing Embedded Computations

A trick in interpreting guidance is always to be alert for embedded or assumed computations. By spotting them and breaking them out early, you can simplify the remaining analysis significantly. (You can also use them to verify and refine your concept model.)

The Cost-Share Policy, for example, assumes the ability to compute 'contribution per family per benefit year' so it can be compared to the $500 threshold. So, a formula for that computation needs to be specified.

Using the concept model diagram as a blueprint, the following (almost practicable) definitional rule can be specified.[17] For convenience, terms in the concept model diagram appear in bold, and wordings for verb concepts appear underlined.

---

[17] A basic RuleSpeak® guideline is to use the term for the number being computed as the subject of the sentence. That approach puts the 'heavy lifting' toward the end of the sentence.

Computation Rule: *The contribution per family per benefit year is computed as the sum of the* ***client fee portion*** *for all approved* ***claims*** *within a benefit year filed for each* ***service event*** *performed for any* ***patient*** *who belongs to the same* ***family****.*

The sentence uses the concept model diagram as a structural blueprint. This may seem like overkill in expressing a single rule. Typical projects involving rules for government and business, however, often involve dozens, hundreds, or even more statements of guidance. Following a structured vocabulary is the price you pay for consistency and coherence across the whole set.

Following a structured vocabulary is the price for consistency and coherence across a set of rules.

Above, I described this rule as 'almost practicable'. What's missing? If you examine the statement carefully, you can identify at least two shortfalls:

- *What is a 'benefit year'?* Timeframes and timing qualifications, of course, are always important. Is it a calendar year? Something else? As it turns out, this organization uses a special benefit year. So, we need to specify a definitional rule:

  Definitional Rule: *A benefit year is July 1 – June 30.*

- *How about 'approved'?* How can you determine whether a given claim is approved? Can we assume we already have some fact (stored data) indicating as much? If so, no additional analysis is needed. If not, what are the criteria (definitional rules) for determining whether a claim is approved? That point of 'drill-down' could lead to a host of additional rules.

Skill 3. Addressing the Core Guidance

Now that we have a rule for computing the contribution per family per benefit year, we can tackle the core issue the policy addresses: How much is the client fee portion for any given claim?

At first, the logic seems simple. The percentage is 25% if the family has not yet exceeded the maximum $500 for the benefit year. It's 0% if the family has.

The difficulty arises when a single claim in a benefit year takes a family over the $500 threshold. In that special case, the actual amount of the client fee portion is (probably) just whatever takes the family up to $500. So, for that claim, the percentage is actually less than 25%, but still greater than 0%.

That interpretation is an assumption. It's *probably* right. It's *probably* just a situation the policy makers didn't foresee or simply assumed would be understood. Nonetheless, the assumption should be verified with them in case they intended (or would want) something else.

Assumptions in interpreting policies should be verified with policy makers.

Assuming the interpretation to be correct, this definitional rule can be expressed as follows. For visibility, the amount computed by the earlier computation rule has been shown in bold.

Client Responsibility Rule: *The client fee portion for an approved claim is the smaller of the following:*

- *25% of the claim amount*
- *$500 minus the* ***contribution per family per benefit year*** *at the time the claim is placed*

Under this logic, the client fee portion is either 25% of the claim amount or whatever amount takes the family over the $500 threshold. If the family has hit the $500 threshold previously, the client fee portion is $0.

Note how addressing the 'embedded' computation rule for 'contribution per family per benefit year' beforehand greatly simplified the rendering and expression of this second rule. If that logic had been embedded in this second rule (rather than simply referenced by name), this second rule would have been much more difficult to capture and the resulting expression far less approachable.

Externalizing computational logic in the manner illustrated by the first rule has important benefits:

- It makes the logic re-usable by other rules not yet analyzed.
- It simplifies the expression of every rule that references it.
- It ensures the same logic is applied consistently everywhere referenced.
- It 'single-sources' the logic in case it changes, thereby improving its maintainability, and thus overall agility.

The rule of thumb is this: Computational logic should not be embedded in a rule if its result can be named and the logic expressed separately in another rule. Following this practice faithfully enhances the overall quality of a set of rules significantly.

Computational logic should not be embedded in a rule if its result can be named and the logic expressed separately in another rule.

Skill 4. Naming and Supporting Thresholds

Central to the Cost Share Policy is the threshold *$500*. Thresholds, of course, are often used in multiple rules. They also have a way of changing over time.

To continue the idea of externalizing logic, two additional steps might be warranted, both to build on the advantages listed above.

1. *Give a name to the threshold.* For example, the $500 threshold might be called the 'maximum contribution per family per benefit year'. The second rule above now would be expressed as follows (with the new threshold name in bold):

   Client Responsibility Rule: *The client fee portion for an approved claim is the smaller of the following:*

   - *25% of the claim amount*
   - *the **maximum contribution per family per benefit year** minus the contribution per family per benefit year at the time the claim is placed*

2. *Establish a means to permit the threshold to vary year-by-year.* One means to support such variability is using a simple decision table, as the following illustrates.

Benefit Year	What is the maximum contribution per family per benefit year?
July 1, 2018 – June 30, 2019	$400
July 1, 2019 – June 30, 2020	$400
July 1, 2020 – June 30, 2021	$475
July 1, 2021 – June 30, 2022	$450
July 1, 2022 – June 30, 2023	$475
July 1, 2023 – June 30, 2024	$500
July 1, 2024 – June 30, 2025	$500
July 1, 2025 – June 30, 2026	$550

Skill 5. Handling Exceptions

A common mistake that policy interpreters and analysts make in addressing guidance is to address exceptions earlier rather than later. It's a real temptation because the exceptions often present meaty challenges. And yes, there are almost always exceptions.

Yes, there are almost always exceptions.

Addressing exceptions earlier rather than later, however, complicates matters significantly. First, adequate vocabulary structure and computational terms are frequently lacking to address them. Second, iteration is always the best way forward. Seldom if ever do you arrive at practicable logic in one giant leap. So, always get a handle on the 'happy cases' (the most routine) first.

Always get a handle on the 'happy cases' first.

And be sure you know what exceptions really are. Many things you might think are exceptions *aren't*. Handling exceptions properly is the subject of Chapter IV-1.

Sure enough, the Cost Share Policy does have an exception.

Cost Share Policy Exception: *Clients who are members of low-income families are exempt from the cost share policy.*

Since this exception represents a policy, it should be treated as a behavioral rule:

Low-Income Family Rule: *A low-income family must not be charged a client fee portion for any claim.*

Then the earlier rule could be adjusted as follows:

Client Responsibility Rule: *The <u>calculated</u> client fee portion for an approved claim is the smaller of the following:*

- *25% of the claim amount*
- *$500 minus the contribution per family per benefit year at the time the claim is placed*
- <u>$0 if the patient belongs to a low-income family</u>

Two revisions have been made:

- The result of the calculation has been renamed *calculated client fee portion* to avoid any conflict with the behavioral rule (Low-Income Family Rule).
- A third conditional clause has been added.

Thank your lucky stars! Exceptions often involve much more complexity that that.

Chapter III-2

Discovery of Flash Points

Consider the No-Shirt, No-Service Rule. Seems like a fairly simple matter to detect potential violations, right? A shirtless customer appears at the entrance to the restaurant and seeks entry; the customer is turned away. Done! *Or is it?!*

Consider the following possibilities. A customer who was shirted upon arrival decides after being seated to remove their shirt. Or the customer goes into the restroom and changes into a non-compliant 'shirt' and returns to dine. It could happen, right? If the restaurant is serious about its rules, it needs to be aware of these potential violations too.

Here then is a fundamentally important insight about behavioral rules. In general, even for the simplest rule, there are *two or more events* when it could potentially be violated.

> *In general, even for the simplest behavioral rule, there are two or more events when it could potentially be violated.*

Aside: Behavioral rules do exist that are specific to a single event, but they represent a small minority. Several examples are presented in Appendix N.

Such potential-violation events are called the rule's *flash points.* Here are the two flash points for the No-Shirt, No-Service Rule:

1. When a customer enters the restaurant to dine.
2. When a customer already seated removes or changes their shirt.

Ever wonder how violations of rules sneak through our business designs? Why processes don't always produce consistent results? How data quality goes awry right at the point of origin?

Here's one big reason: Analysis methods, information systems, process platforms – and current rule platforms – fail to focus on *all* potential-violation events for each behavioral rule. To achieve correctness of results, consistent experience, and high data quality, your approach needs to consider *all* events where each behavioral rule could potentially be violated. Software platforms need to support those events *in real time*.

For correct results, consistent experience, and high data quality, consider all real-time events where each behavioral rule could potentially be violated.

Before looking at more examples, two important points to keep in mind:

- This chapter focuses mostly on behavioral rules and flash points. Definitional rules, however, also have flash points. Those flash points can produce faults of their own. Moreover, a flash point for a definitional rule can often cause some behavioral rule(s) to be violated. For example, suppose a customer already seated in the restaurant rips the sleeves off their shirt such that the garment can no longer counts as a shirt. Refer to Appendix O for additional discussion of flash points and definitional rules.
- The possibility of violations is the central characteristic of behavioral rules. This discussion should be understood, however, in the broader context of shaping behavior. It is quite possible that detecting and rewarding *compliance* with behavioral rules might sometimes be desirable. Refer to Appendix G for brief discussion.

A Simple Example

Even the simplest rules imaginable generally have two flash points. For example:

Address Rule: *A customer must have an address.*

This simple rule also has two flash points:

- When a new customer arises (is created).
- When the address of an existing customer is eliminated (is deleted).

Did you think of that second flash point? It wouldn't make sense to enforce the rule only at the first flash point. Somebody might come along two seconds later and eliminate the customer's address. Such action would clearly subvert the intent of the rule (and the quality of your data).

Why is this distinction between rules and flash points so important? The two or more events where a rule needs to be evaluated are likely to occur within at least two, and possibly many, different processes, procedures, or use cases. They might also occur *anywhere* in ad hoc (unmodeled) business activity.

Yet for all these different processes, procedures, use cases, and other activity, there is only a single rule. By specifying the rule once and only once, then faithfully supporting all its flash points wherever they occur, you ensure consistent experience (and high data quality).

By faithfully supporting all a rule's flash points wherever they occur, you ensure consistent experience (and high data quality).

Discovering and analyzing flash points often also proves very useful in validating rules. Important and sometimes surprising guidance issues often arise.

Starting from declarative rules to identify flash points is not a feature of any traditional requirements or IT methodology. Nor does any widely-used rule platform provide support for identifying and implementing flash points from declarative rules in automated fashion.

> *Aside:* If you're accustomed to thinking in terms of decisions, ask yourself what natural business decision the second flash point corresponds to? The notion of 'decision' adds little or no value to flash points. See Appendix D for additional discussion.

Is it any wonder that legacy systems so often produce such inconsistent (or consistently wrong) results and poor data quality?!

More-Complex Examples

Let's examine two more rules to illustrate flash point discovery. These two rules exhibit about-average or slightly-above-average complexity.

Concept models[18] often prove very helpful for flash point discovery. Each example below is illustrated by a small concept model diagram including only that subset of vocabulary directly relevant to the given rule and its flash points.

More-Complex Example 1

The following rule is for the fictional car rental company EU-Rent.

> Rule: *The reservation holder of a points reservation must be a club member.*

A partial concept model diagram for the vocabulary used in this rule in presented in Figure 1.

[18] Refer to *Business Knowledge Blueprints: Enabling Your Data to Speak the Language of the Business* (2nd ed), by Ronald G. Ross, 2020.

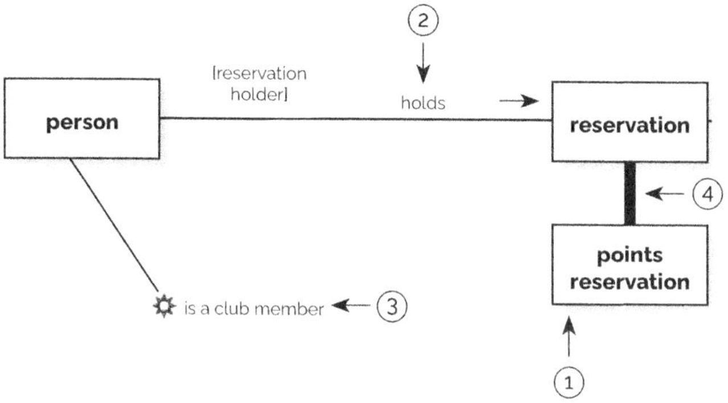

Figure 1. *Concept Model Diagram Supporting Flash-Point Discovery of the EU-Rent Rule*

In the diagram:

- A thick line represents a category (specialization).
- A thin line with a sunburst symbol (labeled 'is a club member') represents a unary verb concept (which evaluates only to true, false, or unknown for any given person).

For convenience the flash points are numbered.
The EU-Rent rule has these four flash points:

1. When a points reservation is created.
2. When the person holding a points reservation is changed.
3. When the reservation holder of a points reservation ceases to be a club member.
4. When an existing reservation is converted into a points reservation.

Unless the rule is evaluated at all four flash points, some violations will be missed. Such omissions have immediate consequences for quality of service, as well as for quality of data. Indeed, such omissions are often root causes of such shortcomings.

More-Complex Example 2

The following rule is from a client that is a distributor of vehicle fuel and associated products.

Rule: *A territory must not include more than one of the following:*

- *Ultra-service.*
- *Food outlet.*
- *Non-candidate traditional gas station.*

A partial concept model diagram for the vocabulary used in this rule is presented in Figure 2. For convenience the flash points are again numbered.

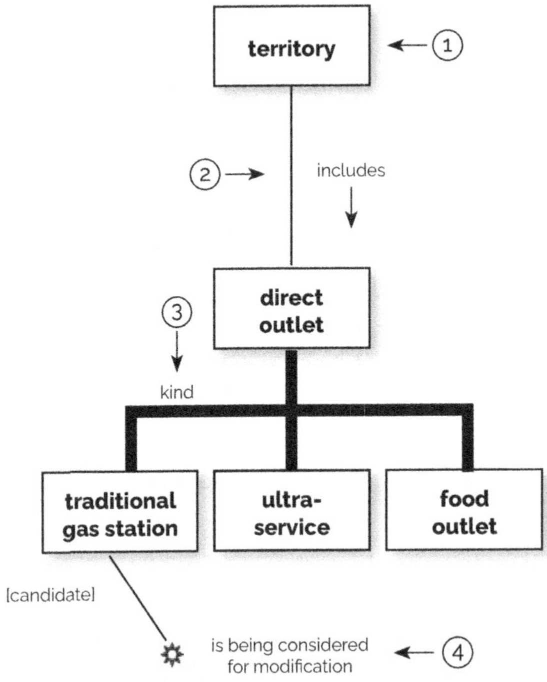

Figure 2. *Concept Model Diagram Supporting Flash-Point Discovery for the Distributor of Vehicle Fuel Rule*

This rule has four flash points, as follows:

1. When a new territory is created (that includes direct outlets).
2. When a direct outlet is included in an existing territory.
3. When the kind of direct outlet already included in a territory is changed.
4. When a traditional gas station already included in a territory is indicated as not being considered for modification (i.e., when indicated as a non-candidate traditional gas station).

Unless the rule is evaluated at all four flash points, some violations will be missed.

Key Points

The examples above illustrate how flash points for rules can be discovered. Smart tools could certainly help!

Lack of automatic support for flash points in current rule platforms has huge implications for programmer workload. For discussion, refer to Appendix P, where an additional example of flash points is presented.

Each of the subset diagrams in the examples above is very limited in scope compared to an entire concept model. This small size reflects an important point about evaluation of rules with respect to data. Compared to evaluation of large sets of inference rules, which is often quite broad in (data) scope, flash-point evaluation for behavioral rules and related definitional rules is usually quite limited in scope.

Although every rule has its own flash points, the same event can be a flash point for multiple rules. (In other words, the relationship of rules and events is many-to-many.) This fact should not be surprising since different rules often pertain to the very same knowledge.

Aside: The conventional wisdom for responding to multiple faults produced by the same event is to detect and respond to the most severe faults first. This is a matter of user friendliness. It can be very frustrating to correct a series of smaller errors, only to then encounter a more severe error that cannot be immediately corrected.

Besides their obvious role in evaluating rules, flash points also play a central role in real-time dissemination of business knowledge. The next chapter explains. *Read on!*

Flash points also play a central role in real-time dissemination of business knowledge.

Chapter III-3

Discovery of Messages

Consider the following three sentences about good hygiene:

1. *Do you cover your mouth when coughing?*

   This sentence is a question, so it cannot be a rule. However, it suggests the possibility of some rule and perhaps could even be used in determining compliance with that rule.

2. *Cover your mouth when you cough.*

   This sentence is an instruction. It communicates that an action should be taken (cover your mouth) in certain circumstances (when you cough). It strongly suggests a rule, but instead of expressing it directly, indicates how to comply with it.

3. *A person who is coughing should cover their mouth.*

   This sentence is a proper rule because all the following are true:

   - It assumes no context (there is a clear antecedent for 'their').
   - It's purely factual, expressing no command or action.
   - The keyword 'should' overtly stamps ruleness.

Refer to Chapters II-2 and II-3 for discussion of these basic criteria for expressing rules.

About Do's and Don'ts

In everyday (informal) communication, people naturally prefer sentence two over sentence three. The guidance is clear and approachable. As an instruction, it tells you exactly what to do. In that respect, it's an effective interpersonal message.

Sentence two could be rephrased as a 'do' (in the sense of *do's and don'ts)*.

Instruction: *Do cover your mouth when you cough.*

We hear and see such *do and don't* messages all the time. Where the context is clear, they are also very effective in communicating guidance informally.

Where the context is clear, do and don't messages are very effective in communicating guidance informally.

For example, you've probably been hearing *do's and don'ts* such as the following in the context of virtual meetings:

- Do check your internet connection and hardware in advance.
- Don't give long answers.
- Do mute yourself while not speaking.
- Don't forget to unmute yourself when starting to speak.

Do's and don'ts are not, however, *formal* rules. Sets of rules need to be expressed in a form that can be verified automatically for consistency and conflicts using logic. Rules in business and government can be exceedingly complex. For formal communication, the distinction between rules and instructions needs to be strictly maintained.[19]

The examples and discussion above suggest we need to probe more deeply into the aspects of guidance conveyed by rules, instructions, and questions. Can their inter-relationships be directly exploited in a productive way? In particular, can questions and instructions play an important role alongside rules? The answer is a resounding *yes*. Read on.

---

19 For more about the distinction between informal and formal communication, refer to *Business Knowledge Messaging: How to Avoid Business Miscommunication*, by Ronald G. Ross, 2022.

Guidance Message(s) for a Rule

The first step in that regard is to broaden our view of instructions. An instruction is just one type of message that can be directly associated with a rule. There are many others.

For example, remember the No-Shirt, No-Service Rule? It wouldn't feel very friendly to be rejected at a restaurant as a consequence of the rule. So, the restaurant would be wise to prepare the hosts with some soothing messaging when enforcing the rule. Maybe, "If it were up to me, I'd let you in, but the owner is a hard case." Or better, "We would be pleased to offer you a low-cost t-shirt that you can take with you." (naturally with the restaurant's name and logo).

The term we use for any message associated with a rule other than the practicable rule statement itself is 'guidance message'.

Flash-Time Messages

Many guidance messages are *flash-time*, meaning they are intended to be disseminated immediately upon evaluation of the associated rule (often but not always upon attempted violation of a behavioral rule). Refer to Chapter III-2 on flash points.

The evaluation of a rule (whether automated or not) always provides an opportunity for additional messages. Such messages can:

- Provide instructions (do's and don'ts) to resolve or avoid the problem.
- Put a friendlier face on an unpleasant or surprising outcome, or provide encouragement.
- Help clarify the result.
- Inform other parties with a need to know.
- Communicate relevant tips and tricks ('help').
- Explain or reinforce the importance of the rule.

Suppose you are exceeding the posted speed limit (a rule). A cop stops you, informs you of the violation, and writes out a citation. This event is likely to be accompanied by some informal messaging in the form of an explanation of why you were stopped, 'a talking to' about the dangers of speeding, a tip about taking defensive driving classes to avoid an increase in insurance premiums, etc. The evaluation of a rule should always be considered a potential teaching moment where relevant knowledge can be disseminated or re-iterated in a timely fashion.

Evaluation of a rule should always be considered a potential teaching moment where relevant knowledge can be disseminated or re-iterated in timely fashion.

Each guidance message should be tailored to the role of the intended recipient (e.g., customer, service representative, supervisor, security officer, compliance officer, etc.). Since guidance messages can often assume context, they can be greatly simplified compared to formal statement of the rule. They also present an opportunity to get creative, using any and all media (e.g., videos) helpful in getting the messaging across.

> *Remember:* Don't forget that the formal statement of a rule is also a message itself in the sense that it communicates guidance from some member(s) of a community to others. If the formal statement is understandable to relevant parties on its own (as is often the case), no additional messaging is necessary.

Pre-Posted Messages

Another kind of guidance message is *pre-posted*. Pre-posted messages are pre-emptive in the sense that they warn you a rule applies and might be enforced. Below are some examples. You can be sure these are guidance messages, not rules, because each assumes context.

- On a fence line: *No Trespassing!*
- In an elevator: *Max 6 Persons.*
- At a security checkpoint: *No photography.*
- On a website form: *Don't hit the back button.*

As these examples illustrate, pre-posted messages are often greatly abbreviated because of limited real estate for messaging (e.g., on a smart phone or physical sign).

Our most familiar example of a pre-posted message is *No Shirt, No Service* at the entrance to the restaurant. The actual rule behind this message (if it ever needed to be properly articulated) is probably the following.

Actual Shirt Rule: *A customer dining in the restaurant must wear a shirt.*

Remember, a message, pre-posted or otherwise, is not necessarily the rule!

A message is not necessarily the rule!

Fact Acquisition Question(s) for a Rule

As discussed earlier, some question(s) can also be associated directly with a rule. They too can have an important supporting role to play. How so? To continue with the No-Shirt, No-Service Rule, suppose a potential customer appears at the entrance to the restaurant. What is needed to evaluate compliance with the rule?

Logically, you need to answer the question *Is this person wearing a shirt?* This case is so simple there's probably no need to verbalize the question explicitly or even recite it mentally, but to enforce the rule the question nonetheless has to be answered. There are two possibilities, both of which can be expressed as facts.

- This person is wearing a shirt.
- This person is not wearing a shirt.

Once the answer is determined, entrance can be allowed or disallowed.

> *Aside:* It's actually not quite that simple. As previously discussed, you also need an understanding of 'shirt'. Depending on how carefully the restaurant wants to maintain its decorum, there could be quite a few definitional criteria (definition and/or definitional rules) for determining whether some article of clothing worn on the upper body of a customer can be considered a 'shirt'.

In Chapter I-2, we examined how every rule should be expressed factually. To convert a well-expressed rule to some question(s) is generally quite straightforward. The more carefully expressed the rule, the more succinct the question(s) will be. The following example illustrates.

> Rule: *A customer must not purchase emergency supplies on credit.*
>
> Inherent Question: *Is a customer purchasing emergency supplies on credit?*

Every natural language has syntax to easily transform a factual expression into a question. The question might be asked in different ways, but all forms of the question seek the same answer.

> *Aside:* The answer for each question is generally binary (yes/no, true/false), but since some relevant fact(s) might be undetermined, 'unknown' must also be accommodated. In other words, an open world is assumed. The real world (as opposed to say database theory) is messy.

Let me make that last point differently. If you can't ask some unambiguous question to evaluate a rule (even if the question is never articulated), then you don't have a practicable rule – and possibly not a rule at all.

If you can't ask some unambiguous question to evaluate a rule, then you don't have a practicable rule – and possibly not a rule at all.

Don't underestimate how powerful this idea is. For example, a platform that 'speaks' rules on a factual basis can rather easily transform those expressions automatically into questions, *always!* Why might that be useful? If relevant facts (data) aren't available, the platform can ask humans ('users') for them.[20] Human evaluators, of course, can do exactly the same thing.

The Rule Messaging Triad

Taken together, the formal statement of a rule, the rule's fact acquisition question(s), and the rule's guidance message(s) comprise the *Rule Messaging Triad*. The Triad applies to both behavioral rules and definitional rules.

The formal statement of a rule, the rule's fact acquisition question(s), and the rule's guidance message(s) comprise the Rule Messaging Triad.

---

20 This ability to 'flip' a rule to ask a question has been exploited for many years by some rule platforms – for example, Oracle Intelligent Advisor (formerly Oracle Policy Automation (OPA)).

The Triad is a powerful device to tie together core bits of business knowledge in a meaningful, manageable way. For example, it can help you organize, communicate, and re-use all your *do-and-don't* messages in a highly scalable way.

The remainder of this chapter presents examples for the Triad. As you review these examples, keep the following points in mind.

- *Rule.* The rule needs to be expressed as completely and as unambiguously as possible. That's how precision is achieved.
- *Fact Acquisition Question(s).* Given a complete and unambiguous expression of the rule, fact acquisition questions can be generated automatically by a machine.
- *Guidance Message(s).* Since the rule should have already been expressed clearly and unambiguously, guidance messages are always optional and supplemental. Multiple guidance messages for the same rule can be expressed for different actors or roles, each following its own style and tone.

In developing or capturing rules, your approach should start with rules, then customize guidance messages (if any) around those rules. Don't put the cart before the horse. An iterative approach, however, is fine. In many cases, you may actually come across the guidance messages first.

The Triad for Definitional Rules: Examples

EU-Rent has the following definitional rule.

Definitional Rule: *A reservation always requests a car group.*

Table 1 presents the associated fact acquisition questions and sample guidance message for this definitional rule.

Table 1. *Rule Messaging Triad Applied to EU-Rent Definitional Rule*

	Definitional Rule	Fact Acquisition Question	Sample Guidance Message
Reservation Rule	A reservation always requests a car group.	What car group is requested for the reservation?	Please request a car group for your reservation. Otherwise, we will be unable to complete your reservation.

In Chapter I-3, the (definitional) What's-a-Shirt Rule was specified to support the (behavioral) No-Shirt, No-Service Rule. Table 2 presents the associated fact acquisition questions and sample guidance messages for that definitional rule.

Table 2. *Rule Messaging Triad Applied to the What's-a-Shirt Rule*

	Definitional Rule	Fact Acquisition Questions	Sample Guidance Message
What's-a-Shirt Rule	A shirt has sleeves and a tail long enough to be tucked inside the waistband of trousers or a skirt.	Does the shirt have sleeves? Does the shirt have a tail long enough to be tucked inside the waistband of trousers or a skirt? Don't call something a shirt if the answer to any of these questions is no.	Don't call something a shirt if the answer to any of these questions is no.

Refer to Appendix C (at the end) for discussion of applying the Rule Messaging Triad to decision tables.

The Triad for Behavioral Rules: Examples

Table 3 presents a subset of behavioral rules for the fictional car rental company EU-Rent. Fact acquisition questions and sample guidance messages are also included for each rule, all using consistent vocabulary.[21]

Table 3. *Rule Messaging Triad Applied to EU-Rent Behavioral Rules*

	Behavioral Rule	Fact Acquisition Question	Sample Guidance Message
Reservation Rules	A reservation must indicate an intended pick-up branch.	Which pick-up branch is intended for the reservation?	We need to know where you'd like to pick up your rental car.
	The reservation holder of a points reservation must be a club member.	Is the reservation holder of the points reservation a club member?	Points reservations are restricted to club members. Refer to our website about becoming a club member and see all the benefits you can enjoy.
Car Pick-Up Rules	The rental car that is assigned to a rental must be located at the actual pick-up branch of the rental at the pick-up date-time of the rental	Is the rental car assigned to the rental located at the actual pick-up branch of the rental at the pick-up date-time of the rental?	Urgent: Assign a different rental car suitable for this reservation.

21 The vocabulary and concept model diagram for EU-Rent are presented in *Business Knowledge Blueprints: Enabling Your Data to Speak the Language of the Business* (2nd ed), by Ronald G. Ross, 2020, Appendix 3.

	Behavioral Rule	Fact Acquisition Question	Sample Guidance Message
Rental Rules	A rental may result from a reservation only if the renter who is responsible for that rental is the reservation holder of that reservation.	Does the renter responsible for the rental hold the reservation?	We're sorry. The renter financially responsible for the rental must have made the reservation.
	A rental charge may be charged against a credit card only if the credit card is held by the renter who is responsible for the rental that incurs the rental charge.	Is the credit card against which the rental charge is being charged held by the renter who is responsible for the rental?	Never charge for a rental using any credit card not held by the renter responsible for the rental.
	A rental may be open only if a provisional rental charge that is incurred for that rental is charged against a credit card that is held by the renter of that rental.	Is the provisional rental charge for the open rental charged against a credit card held by the renter?	An open rental requires a provisional rental charge against the renter's credit card.
	A rental must incur a penalty charge if the drop-off branch of the rental is not the pick-up branch of the rental.	Is the drop-off branch of the rental different from the pick-up branch of that rental?	Since you have not returned your rental car to the same branch where you picked it up, we must charge a drop-off fee.

Postscript: The examples of guidance messages in this table are mostly focused on violations since the possibility of violations is the central characteristic of behavioral rules. Guidance messages should be understood, however, in the broader context of shaping behavior. It is quite possible that acknowledging and rewarding *compliance* with behavioral rules might sometimes be desirable. Refer to Appendix G for brief discussion.

Part III Summary

Analyzing Rules

With rules, you're always on a journey of discovery – discovery of the rules themselves, discovery of the rules' flash points, and discovery of messages associated with the rules.

Interpretation of source materials to produce practicable rules in business and government requires five basic skills:

1. Developing business vocabulary
2. Capturing embedded computations
3. Addressing the core guidance
4. Naming and supporting thresholds
5. Handling exceptions

Gaps and open issues in policies are inevitable. Those must be sorted out. Following a structured vocabulary based on a concept model is the price for consistency and coherence across a set of rules. Assumptions in interpreting source materials should be verified with policy makers or other subject matter experts.

A rule is a rule. A flash point is a flash point. They shouldn't be confused. Flash points are real-time events in business activity that attempt to change something relevant to one or more rules. In general, even the simplest rule has two or more flash points. To achieve correct results, consistent experience, and high data quality, consider *all* flash points where each rule could potentially be violated.

Flash points also play a central role in real-time dissemination of business knowledge. Evaluation of a rule should be considered a potential teaching moment where relevant knowledge can be disseminated in timely fashion.

Where the context is clear, *do-and-don't* messages are very effective in informally communicating guidance. A more comprehensive approach involves coordinating all the following for rules:

- Formal statement(s)
- Fact acquisition question(s)
- Guidance message(s)

This unifying threesome for rules is called the *Rule Messaging Triad.*

Part IV

Rule Quality

A set of rules has high rule quality if it is free of surprises. I don't mean surprises in the sense of "Wow! I didn't know we had that rule!" Or, "Wow! I didn't know *that's* what we meant!"

Rather, I mean surprises in the sense of irregularities, inconsistencies, conflicts, or misdirection. The work people perform is detailed and sometimes highly sensitive. It does not need to be complicated by rules expressed in non-intuitive or defective ways. Every rule statement should be fully trustworthy in its own right.

Every rule statement should be fully trustworthy in its own right.

To prepare for this discussion of rule quality, Part II explained how individual rules are best expressed. Part III took us on a journey of discovery in capturing and analyzing individual rules. Now it's time to analyze *sets* of rules to ensure they 'play' together well. This Part examines three areas in that regard:

- Exceptions. *How should you think about exceptions? What's the best way to handle them?*
- Anomalies. *What kind of irregularities or inconsistencies can be found across sets of rules? What's the best way to resolve them?*
- Knock-out rules. *How do you handle behavioral rules with respect to decision tables? How do you avoid needless complexity in decision tables?*

This discussion will leave you well-equipped to produce high-quality sets of rules. That way you can ensure highly-consistent results in organizational activities – and high-quality data as well.

Before diving in, however, let me re-emphasize a crucial point. Rules have high quality if and only if they organize interactions between people and communities properly. If the expression of rules gets tangled up with the means of their implementation, proper support will be very hard to evaluate. Entanglement of rules with software platforms in particular is a classic mistake.

Let's be clear what I mean by 'entanglement'. These days we all depend increasingly on technology. So of course, you can have rules *for* technology. And *about* technology. And in *regard to* technology. That's not what I mean by 'entanglement'.

Stakeholders of rules in business and government should always be able to read rule expressions and, if they understand the vocabulary (even if about technologies), not worry about anything else. They should never have to care how software developers solve platform problems, interface problems, display problems, or any other problems that result from software, data, or technical architectures. *Why should they?!*

The rules needed to coordinate groups and communities of people are often complex in their own right. For the sake of all the non-developers in the world (which is most people), as well as those who are developers, keep rules strictly disentangled from implementation code. Actually, that's often half the battle over matters of rule quality.

For the sake of all the non-developers in the world (which is most people) keep rules strictly disentangled from implementation code.

Chapter IV-1

Exceptions

I've heard people say that for every rule they have 10 exceptions. I respond, "No, you have *eleven* rules." That's not an exact count (probably too high), but it does make the point. Often, an exception to a rule is just another rule.

Then allow myself a small digression, which I'll also take here.[22] Bear with me.

- Generally, more behavioral rules is *not* better.
- Usually, fewer *good* behavioral rules is better, just enough to provide adequate guardrails against significant risks and to deliver consistent business results.

Remember, no rule is a free lunch. Each behavioral rule costs something to create and deploy. Even if automated, people who bump into it must learn it. So, be sure:

- The rule is properly motivated by business goals and objectives.
- The cost of the rule's enforcement is balanced against the risks it protects you from, and the opportunities that enforcement may cause you to lose.

(End of digression.)

Many organizations have overly abundant behavioral rules. Why? Perhaps the organization has not thought through its policies carefully enough (or for whatever reason prefers not to). Or because lots of outdated legacy rules lurk in the byways ('zombie' rules). Or too many lawyers in the kitchen. These are all matters of good business governance.

---

22 Up to "end of digression" these points are based directly on the *Business Rule Manifesto*, Article 8, 2003. https://www.brcommunity.com/brg/BRManifesto.pdf

No matter what the reason, overabundance significantly complicates sets of rules – not to mention everyday business activity(!).

Overabundance significantly complicates sets of rules – not to mention everyday business activity.

Apart from issues of good business governance, the two most common sources of unnecessary abundance and complexity in sets of rules are counting the wrong things as exceptions and handling true exceptions wrong. Let's start this discussion by examining these two important issues.

Counting the Wrong Things as Exceptions

Often what people (especially software developers) see as an exception is not really an exception at all. This misperception can arise in several ways, as follows.

Often what people see as an exception to a rule is not really an exception at all.

Enforcement Level

Often, differential enforcement of a behavioral rule is desirable so as to allow real-time insertion of sentiment, human discretion, and common sense into ongoing business activity. So, the enforcement level for a behavioral rule might vary from 'strictly enforced' to mere 'guideline'.

Consider a workplace No-Hugs-For-Co-Workers Rule. If a co-worker is choking to death and needs the Heimlich Maneuver, you'd want to over-ride that rule. A rule with an enforcement level that allows overrides does *not* produce exceptions! Refer to Chapter I-4 and Appendix H for additional discussion of enforcement level.

A rule with an enforcement level that allows overrides does not produce exceptions.

Applicability Conditions

Often, the very same behavioral rule has different enforcement levels depending on the situation or circumstances (e.g., location, time of day, the state of some business interaction, etc.). Applicability conditions allow you to specify the underlying rule only once. Consider the following example:

Health-Insurance Rule: *The amount claimed for a sling must be less than or equal to the special limit for an incidental if all the following are true:*

- *the claimant is out-of-state*
- *the claim amount is less than or equal to $500.*

This very same rule might be relevant both in responding to customer inquiries and in validating actual claims.

- *For customer inquiries ("Would I be covered if ... ?"):* Enforcing the rule strictly is inappropriate (meaningless). Here, the rule merely acts as a guideline in assessing hypothetical situations.
- *For actual claims.* Enforcing the rule strictly is appropriate. Here, outright denial of claims is the probable result.

Different applicability conditions (with distinct enforcement levels) for the very same behavioral rule are *not* exceptions! Refer to Chapter I-4 for more about applicability conditions.

Different applicability conditions with distinct enforcement levels for the very same behavioral rule are not exceptions!

Knock-Out Rules

Decision tables are often rife with entries attempting to support 'exceptions'. Such entries are a significant reason why decision tables used on their own (without protective behavioral rules) can become so complex.

For example, if you are underage or a felon, your mortgage application is probably never going to be approved no matter what. Why work that logic into decision tables for deciding whether to approve an applicant's mortgage? In such cases, the 'normal' decision logic doesn't need to be evaluated at all.

Not being underage or a felon aren't exceptions to the 'normal' decision logic. Those are hard-and-fast behavioral rules about rejecting mortgage applications. We call them *knock-out rules*. A knock-out rule is *not* an exception! See Chapter IV-3 for additional discussion and illustration of knock-out rules.

Knock-out rules for decision logic are not exceptions.

Authorizations

An authorization is an explicit permission given by some authority that allows activity that otherwise would be prohibited. Authorizations involve use of resources that are deemed especially sensitive, dangerous, scarce, privileged, and/or valuable. For example, suppose a city decides the peace and quiet of a park is a scarce and valuable resource. Vehicles are noisy, so it enacts the following rule:[23]

Park Rule: *No vehicles in the park.*

23 This rule has been explored extensively in legal literature, including: Bennett Moses LK, 2007, "Recurring Dilemmas: The Law's Race to Keep Up with Technological Change," *University of Illinois Journal of Law, Technology and Policy*, vol. Fall, pp. 239-285.

But logically *some* vehicles have to be allowed in the park – for example, emergency vehicles and park maintenance vehicles. As Chapter V-2 discusses, such special cases can be explicitly authorized in advance. Formally, the result is authorizations, not exceptions.

Special cases authorized in advance are not exceptions.

Handling True Exceptions Wrong

A true exception to a rule occurs when allowance is made for a *foreseen, explicit* set of circumstances in which different-than-normal guidance is to be followed. An example is seeing-eye dogs as an exception to dogs not being allowed in a hospital.

A true exception to a rule allows for a foreseen, explicit set of circumstances in which different-than-normal guidance is to be followed.

Aside: Unforeseen 'exceptions' are handled by appropriate enforcement level. They require injection of sentiment, human discretion, and common sense.

How should true exceptions be handled? There's more to this question than initially meets the eye. Consider the following two warehouse access rules.

General Access Rule: *A customer may have access to the warehouse only during regular business hours.*

Gold Customer Access Rule: *A gold customer must be allowed access to the warehouse at all hours.*

Suppose a gold customer shows up at the warehouse after hours. Should staff let the gold customer in or not? Which rule 'wins'? Is the latter rule meant to be an exception to the former rule? How would staff know?

Staff wouldn't! Some staff might interpret the rules one way; other staff the opposite. Staff who resolve the dilemma inappropriately could feel any reprimands unjust. Gold customers who expected entry could leave quite annoyed. *Houston, we have a problem!*

How is the matter resolved? The key is remembering the purpose of rules for communities and groups of people. The issue is not programming bots, or mimicking intelligent behavior. It's first and foremost about communicating expectations for behavior, then enforcing those expectations.

The purpose of rules for communities and groups of people is communicating expectations for behavior, then enforcing them.

As a result, hidden semantics of any kind in expressing behavioral rules is not a good idea. Clever 'hidden hands' to make rules work right might be acceptable for bots, but not for people (whether the rules can be automated or not). So, here are several approaches that do *not* work well for handling exceptions:

- *Hidden priority schemes.* Suppose the Gold Customer Access Rule is given a seven on a scale of 10. The General Access Rule is given a four. So, seven 'wins' over four, right? But *why?!* Where did these priorities come from? How are they measured? Do staff really have to compare priorities to see which rule 'wins'?! For people, the approach is mysterious and impractical.
- *Category schemes.* 'Gold customer' seems to be a category of customer. So, one could argue that 'gold customer' rules should 'win' over regular 'customer' rules because gold customers are special. *Or,* you could argue the

reverse. 'Customer rules' are more general and therefore should 'win' over any rules for specific categories. Actually, there's no compelling argument either way. More importantly, why should anyone have to remember such conventions in reading what rules say?!

- *Preemptive rule(s).* Some other explicit rule(s) could be specified whose effect is to overturn the original rule. For example:

  The General Access Rule is not to be enforced for gold customers.

  The (big) problem with this solution is the issue of trust. Now you can't read the General Access Rule by itself and trust exactly what it says. This other rule 'undoes' it for gold customers. How would you know this other rule exists? Why would you ever expect such 'over-ride' rules? For people, loss of trust in what they see in front of them is a major issue.

Aside: Phrases such as "notwithstanding anything to the contrary" (all too common in contracts) should never be used in expressing practicable rules. In effect, the phrase creates a self-declared over-ride.

To apply the rules correctly under any of the above approaches, you need to know more than just what each statement says. Semantics are hidden, or at least external. *Not good!*

Clever 'hidden hands' to make rules work right might be acceptable for bots, but not for people.

Handling True Exceptions Right

A basic principle for expressing rules for groups and communities of people is that you should always be able to trust exactly what you read, whatever is right in front of you, at *face value.* (All rules depend on definitions of terms and definitional rules, of course, so this principle assumes the vocabulary is familiar or accessible to the reader.) A rule statement is *face-value trustworthy* if a reader can fully trust exactly what the statement says on its own.

You should always be able to trust exactly what a rule expresses, whatever is right in front of you, at face value.

In other words, each rule can be taken *literally* to mean what it actually says – no more, no less. Apart from definitions and definitional rules, nothing else needs to be known or read.

A direct consequence of this face-value principle is the following: *Any rule statement whose meaning seems to conflict with some other rule statement(s) (or even some other part of the same statement) must be interpreted as conflicting.*

In other words, if by taking some statements(s) literally you find that a potential conflict could arise, you are right – *it can*. And you need to fix it. Potential conflicts must be resolved explicitly, within the actual statement(s).

If by taking some statements(s) literally you find that a potential conflict could arise, you are right – it can.

The real problem with the two warehouse access rules above is that they are in conflict *at face value*. One or the other rule needs to be restated to iron out the conflict.

Which one? The answer depends entirely on business practice. So, ask which of the following represents the correct or desired guidance?

- *Warehouse access is to be restricted for non-gold customers to regular business hours, but not for gold customers.*

- *Warehouse access for all customers, including gold customers, is to be restricted to regular business hours.*

Let's assume the desired business practice is represented by the former statement. So, the two rules jointly representing the correct business practices for warehouse access are the following. The underlined text in the first rule represents a new qualification added to accommodate and resolve the conflict appropriately.

General Access Rule: *A customer that is not a gold customer may have access to the warehouse only during regular business hours.*

Gold Customer Access Rule: *A gold customer must be allowed access to the warehouse at all hours.*

Aside: An even better resolution of the conflict is presented in Chapter V-3, after the notion of rights is introduced.

Back to Informal vs. Formal Communication

Examining the two resulting rules above, now ask yourself: Which is an exception?! Both? Neither? In the sense that each rule statement is now face-value trustworthy (no longer in conflict), the question is not really meaningful. Both now are simply well-expressed rules. Indeed, there is no such thing as an exception in fully formal business communication.

There is no such thing as an exception in fully formal business communication.

Aside: Laws, legal agreements, contracts, etc. tend to be highly formal, of course, but they have one big advantage. The 'four corners' of the document establish a context. Once rules are extracted or interpreted from these documents, and let loose onto the organization as a whole, this original context is easily lost (even if traceability to the source is maintained). To play properly, *every* rule statement needs to be face-value trustworthy no matter what its source.

In informal business communication, of course, we talk about 'exceptions' to rules all the time. For example, we might say: *Customers are to have access to the warehouse only during regular business hours.* Then, later in the same conversation or message we might add: *By the way, none of what we've said earlier applies to gold customers.*

Well-expressed statements of rules for groups and communities of people, however, should not be informal in that sense. You can never be sure when or where some guidance might be read or what the reader's assumptions might be. So, each rule needs to express its full meaning *at face value*. In the process, the notion of 'exception' simply falls over the transom.

Suppose your guidance knowledgebase (rulebook) is deemed free of conflicts and you understand the business vocabulary correctly. If your guidance is well-expressed, then:

- Every statement is always self-explanatory. No need to appeal to any other statement should ever arise in understanding its meaning.
- Every statement can always be taken literally at face value. Take it out of conversational context and you can still trust exactly what it says.

Chapter IV-2

Anomalies

When is the worst possible time to find irregularities or inconsistencies (anomalies) among your rules? It's at points where people, groups, or communities interact 'live' (including digitally).

The worst possible time to find anomalies in rules is when people interact 'live' (including digitally).

Anomalies among rules that surface during interactions almost always have negative consequences, sometimes dire ones. For example:

- At a point of sale, a customer who feels overcharged is likely to be unhappy and vocal. Everyone else in line will be delayed while the issue is resolved. Matter of life and death? *No.* Poor customer experience? *Definitely.*
- Getting vaccinated against a pandemic could *literally* be a matter of life or death. I certainly want the best possible rules *before* I get to that interaction!

High-quality rules are the lubricant that allows business and government, using all manner of technologies, to run smoothly and safely. (Low-quality rules, in contrast, can result in long-running court battles.) Any problems among rules should be identified and *resolved* before live interactions. And bots should be helping to ensure logical consistency(!). (For more, refer to Appendix B.)

High-quality rules are the lubricant that allows business and government to run smoothly and safely.

Rules and business knowledge are complex and extensive – and growing exponentially. So, before looking at the specific kinds of anomalies you can find in sets of behavioral rules and related definitional rules, allow me another quick digression to put the matter into perspective.

1. *Anomalies Are (Almost) Inevitable.* No matter how hard you try, anomalies almost always arise in even relatively small sets of rules. Problems are inevitable when multiple people are involved, working over extended periods of time, with multiple goals at play (often conflicting). No need to beat yourself up about it. Just find the problems.
2. *Rules Are Not to Blame.* There is absolutely nothing (*nothing*!) about rules that somehow causes anomalies to occur. There have *always* been anomalies in the logic that business and governments produce. Why do you think legacy code is often so bad?! Historically most automated rules have been implemented in procedural code where spotting many anomalies is nearly impossible. At least with declarative rules, you have a fighting chance to find them more easily.
3. *But You'll Need Vocabulary.* In one way or another, many anomalies are a matter of vocabulary. Coordinating your vocabulary very carefully in expressing rules is crucial. Remember too, you will probably have lots and lots of rules. Basic coherence across large numbers of rules arises only from consistent use of vocabulary. For these reasons, we always express rules using a structured business vocabulary based on a concept model.[24]

(End of digression.)

[24] Refer to *Business Knowledge Blueprints: Enabling Your Data to Speak the Language of the Business* (2nd ed), by Ronald G. Ross, 2020.

Conflicts

A conflict is an anomaly within or among some rule(s) such that multiple states or outcomes are required that cannot all be satisfied simultaneously. The rule(s) directly and completely contradict each other. Example:

Rule 1: *A high-priced, fragile item must be picked up by the customer.*

Rule 2: *A high-priced, fragile item must be shipped by an insured carrier.*

It is impossible for an item to be picked up by a customer if it is shipped, and vice versa.

> *A conflict is an anomaly within or among some rule(s) such that multiple states or outcomes are required that cannot all be satisfied simultaneously.*

Outright conflicts such as the above cannot be allowed to stand. They 'break' logic. One or the other rule (or both) must be modified.

Aside: Enforcement level should not be used for resolving this kind of conflict. The problem is with the logic, not enforcement.

Vocabulary. Vocabulary is always highly relevant to identifying and resolving conflicts. For example, suppose a restaurant posts the following rule:

Rule: *Gratuities appreciated, but no tips please.*

Whether this rule contradicts itself is entirely bound up in the definitional criteria for 'tip' and 'gratuity'.

Aside: As this example possibly suggests, rules and permissions can also be in conflict. Refer to Chapter V-1 for discussion.

Unintended Block-Outs. Sometimes rules do not completely contradict each other, but do block one another in ways that were probably not intended. Example:

Rule 1: A shipment must include at least 3 orders.

Rule 2: An out-of-state shipment must not include more than 1 order.

As currently expressed, rule 1 is unqualified, so it must be taken to apply to *all* shipment destinations, including those out-of-state. Rule 2, however, permits at most only one order on an out-of-state shipment. The only way both rules can be satisfied is never to allow any out-of-state shipments at all. In other words, out-of-state shipments have been 'blocked out', probably unintentionally.

This example quite possibly reflects an unresolved 'exception' where Rule 2 is meant as an exception to Rule 1. (Refer to Chapter IV-1.) If so, Rule 1 as currently expressed is not *face-value trustworthy*. Assuming Rule 1 applies only to 'in-state' shipments, it must say so.

Revised Rule 1: *An in-state shipment must include at least 3 orders.*

Now, the conditions expressed by the two rules are mutually exclusive (in-state vs. out-of-state) so no shipment destination is blocked out. Also, each rule statement is now fully face-value trustworthy.

Remember: Enforcement level should not be used for resolving this kind of anomaly. The problem is with the logic, not enforcement.

Subsumption

A subsumption in rules is an anomaly where the rules all require or disallow the same state, except that one rule requires or disallows the state for a broader set of circumstances than the other rule. Example:

Rule 1. *A rush order must have a destination.*

Rule 2. *An order must have a destination.*

The first rule is subsumed by the second rule and therefore should be eliminated. That is, the second rule covers all possible circumstances (and more) where the first rule might need to be evaluated. (Subsumption is sometimes considered a form of redundancy.)

A subsumption is an anomaly among rules that all require or disallow the same state, except that one rule covers a broader set of circumstances.

Over Specialization. Sometimes a rule could be subsumed by another rule, but the other rule has not been specified even though more appropriate. Example:

Rule: *Thou shalt not kill <u>with a knife</u>.*

Murder, of course, is not permitted with a gun either. Or poison. Or an automobile. Or anything else.

The rule includes the needless condition 'with a knife', which has the effect of making the rule's coverage too narrow. The rule should be revised.

Revised Rule: *Thou shalt not kill.*

Categories. Sometimes the same rule is specified for each category of a concept. For example, suppose the following three rules are specified:

Rule 1: A <u>silver</u> customer must have a contact method.

Rule 2: A <u>gold</u> customer must have a contact method.

Rule 3: A <u>platinum</u> customer must have a contact method.

Silver, gold, and platinum represent three categories of customer based on loyalty level. Suppose there are no other categories in this scheme (or if there are, an equivalent rule applies). There is no need for three (or more) rules because they can all be subsumed into a single rule:

Subsuming Rule: *A customer must have a contact method.*

Aside: In decision tables, eliminating such subsumptions is called *contraction*.

Redundancy

Ideally, each rule should be expressed once and only once in an authoritative source, and disseminated from there. If the same rule appears more than once in the authoritative source, the risk is that any revision will not be faithfully propagated to all copies, resulting in loss of consistency. We call this notion 'single-sourcing' for rules. Note that the notion pertains to managing rules, not necessarily deploying or automating them.

The risk with redundant rules is that revisions will not be faithfully propagated to all copies.

Assuming use of controlled natural language to express rules, redundancy can arise for several subtle reasons.

Linguistic Equivalence. Redundant rules can arise because of different syntax or form. Example:

Rule 1: *The sum total of an order must not exceed $10,000.*

Rule 2: *The total amount of an order must not be greater than $10,000.*

Presumably, these rules mean the same thing (though that equivalence should be validated). One version can therefore be eliminated, or the two versions indicated as synonymous forms for the same underlying meaning.

The grammar of natural language (even controlled) is flexible, so linguistic equivalence can easily occur. Example:

Rule 1: *A permanent employee must receive a salary.*

Rule 2: *An employee who is permanent must receive a salary.*

Aside: If 'natural language' is completely controlled, the result is essentially a programming language. But why try to turn all rule makers into coders?! First, it is almost certainly hopeless. Second, machines are so powerful these days, and so smart about natural language, surely they can meet up with us at some convenient midpoint!

Reversed Subjects. In certain cases (but by no means all), the subject and object in rule statements can be reversed with no change in meaning. Such rules must of course pertain to exactly the same terms and facts. Example:

Rule 1: *An auditor must not audit any manager in the same city.*

Rule 2: *A manager must not be audited by any auditor in the same city.*

The subject and object are reversed in these two rules, but the meaning of the rules is equivalent. One version can therefore be eliminated, or the two versions indicated as synonymous forms for the same underlying meaning.

As the above example illustrates, 'reversal' equivalence can occur when two or more facts must or must not be the same (i.e., the city of the auditor being the same as the city of the manager). It can also occur when two or more things cannot exist or be true simultaneously. Example:

Rule 1. *A high-risk customer must not place a rush order.*

Rule 2. *A rush order must not be placed by a high-risk customer.*

If a customer is high-risk, any order that customer places must not be rush, and vice versa. Those two facts cannot hold true at the same time.

Modal Equivalence. A rule expressed as a restricted permission can always be expressed as a prohibition and vice versa. This equivalence is dictated by modal logic. Example:

> Rule Expressed as a Restricted Permission: *An employee is permitted an employment counselor only if the employee is not retired.*

> Rule Expressed as a Prohibition: *A retired employee must not have an employment counselor.*

Again, one version can be eliminated, or the two versions indicated as synonymous forms for the same underlying meaning.

Neither form is innately better than the other; however, the grammar of a natural language may prefer one form over the other in certain cases. Example:

> Rule Expressed as a Prohibition: *A person must not smoke if not outdoors.*

> Rule Expressed as a Restricted Permission: *A person is permitted to smoke only if outdoors.*

English frowns on double negatives, so in this case the restricted permission is preferred. For more about forms of expression for rules refer to Appendix M.

Near Identicals. Two or more rules that obligate or prohibit the same kind of fact can be inconsistent about relevant qualifications. Example:

> Rule 1: *A programmer trainee must not maintain a system evaluated at more than $100K.*

> Rule 2: *A system evaluated at more than $100K must not be maintained by a junior programmer.*

Rule 3: *A programmer must not be a trainee if he/she maintains any system evaluated at over $50K.*

Rule 4: *A system must not be evaluated at more than $75K if any of the programmers who maintain the system is a trainee.*

All four of these rules pertain to the basic fact *programmers maintain systems*. Specific qualifications, however, vary. For example, Rule 2 indicates junior programmer instead of trainee. Rules 1 and 2 indicate $100K, whereas Rule 3 indicates $50K and Rule 4 indicates $75K. These rules are similar enough that they should be scrutinized for possible consolidation.

Problems like these are inevitable when multiple people are involved, working over extended periods of times, with multiple goals at play (often conflicting).

Incompleteness

Are rule(s) missing? Are there gaps or holes in coverage? Completeness of sets of rules means there are no gaps or holes in coverage.

Completeness of rules means there are no gaps or holes in coverage.

Unfortunately, there is really no mechanistic way to test the completeness of rules (except those within decision tables, more or less). Ensuring the completeness of a set of rules is largely a matter of digging and 'pulling the threads' (see Chapter III-1). Here are some tips and tricks that can help.

- Applying *pattern questions* is useful. Rules can focus on any of the six interrogatives – *what, how, where, who, when,* and *why*. Over the years we have developed comprehensive, analyst-friendly pattern questions to ask based on those six question words.[25]

[25] *Building Business Solutions: Business Analysis with Business Rules* (2nd Ed.), by Ronald G. Ross with Gladys S.W. Lam, 2015.

- Identifying and exploring edge cases is important. For example, suppose a company has rules about retirement benefits where company contributions are based on years elapsed since an employee joined the company. But how does the company treat an employee who transferred from a different company (e.g., a subsidiary) in the same corporate group? The special rules for this edge case makes a big difference to the employees involved and can have substantial financial impact for the company.
- Examining *thresholds* closely can reveal gaps. For example:

  Rule 1. *The daily rate for an employee must be $10 if the employee is younger than 18 years old.*

  Rule 2. *The daily rate for an employee must be $20 if the employee is older than 18 years* old.

  What about employees who are *exactly* 18 years old?
- Analyzing *flash points* often helps uncover missing policy considerations. Refer to Chapter III-2.
- Running through *activity scenarios* (both normal and exceptional) can be helpful to ensure all significant risks (and opportunities) are covered. Test scenarios can be retained so prior results can be compared with new results for modified rule sets.
- Reviewing *permissions* can be useful. Refer to Chapter V-1. Example:

  Permission: *An order $1,000 or less is permitted on credit without a credit check.*

  A missing rule might be:

  Rule: *An order over $1,000 on credit is prohibited without a credit check.*

Remember: A concept model as expressed in the form of a structured business vocabulary is a natural blueprint to the underlying knowledge. Rely on it for structure and discovery in pursuing completeness.

A final word of advice for assessing completeness: *Don't trust legacy systems(!).* They represent past interpretations (and perhaps many patches since) by software developers who probably didn't fully understand the policies, took shortcuts forced by implementation tools, or were simply in a hurry. Search for authoritative source documents and/or consult knowledgeable policy makers or experts.

Don't trust legacy systems(!).

Chapter IV-3

Knock-Out Rules

Decision tables are often rife with entries attempting to support 'exceptions'. Such entries are a major reason why decision tables used on their own (without protective behavioral rules) become so complex.

Unnecessary complexity in decision tables is another significant issue in rule quality. It's a problem you can avoid. This chapter shows how.

Decision tables are often rife with entries attempting to support 'exceptions'.

Setting the Stage

Let's quickly review the two fundamental kinds of rules.

- *Behavioral rules* are ones that people or processes that represent or support them can violate. Think laws, regulations, contracts, service level agreements, policies, etc. They are about coordinating behavior in groups or communities of people. (See Chapter I-4.)
- *Definitional rules* pertain to forming concepts. Definitional rules cannot be broken; they indicate how things have to be understood. (See Chapter I-5.)

Decision tables involve inference rules, a specific variety of definitional rules. Inference rules imply new facts from existing facts, able to support what is commonly called *inference*.

Decision tables involve inference rules, a specific variety of definitional rules.

Reminder: Behavioral rules *never* support inference, even if conditional (i.e., include an 'if' clause). Refer to Appendix Q (at end).

Do behavioral rules and the rules in decision tables ever cross paths? Yes, all the time. What happens when they do? Which rules 'win'? Understanding this question brings significant clarity to how your business logic should work – and surprisingly, to why your decision tables are often needlessly complex.

Example

Let's consider a relatively simple example. Suppose a city is operating its recreational facilities and needs to assess usage fees. It has created a decision table to determine appropriate usage fees based on length of usage and when the usage occurs, as follows.

What recreational fee should be charged for use of facilities?	***When does the usage occur?***			
How long is the usage?		**weekday**	**weekend during off hours**	**weekend during peak hours**
	< 1 hour	**$2**	**$3**	**$8**
	1-2 hours	**$3**	**$5**	**$10**
	> 2 hours	**$5**	**$8**	**$15**

The decision table is actually a set of inference rules, specifically nine of them (represented by the intersection cells with dollar amounts in them). These nine rules could, of course, have been written out as nine individual statements. For example, the rule represented in the lower right-most cell could have been written as follows:

Rule: *The recreational fee for use of facilities is $15 if on a weekend during peak hours and for more than 2 hours.*

With a well-formed decision table such as the above, however, there is no need to write out the individual rules – a huge advantage since decision tables often involve a large number of rules. Refer to Appendix C for more on decision tables.

Now the wrinkle. As it turns out, the city already has a long-standing policy regarding fee-free use of facilities by senior citizens.

Behavioral Rule: *A senior citizen must not be charged a recreational fee for use of facilities.*

In the case of senior citizens, this behavioral rule is in direct conflict with *all* the rules in the decision table. A senior citizen is never to be charged a recreational fee no matter what the circumstances of usage. So, which rule 'wins' in any given case of usage by a senior citizen? Let's consider each of the two possible answers.

Possible Answer 1.
The Rules in the Decision Table Should Win

Let's suppose the city wants the rules in the decision table to override the behavioral rule. (That seems a bit odd in this example, but no matter for this discussion.) No problem. Definitional rules *always* win over behavioral rules. Period.

Remember: Definitional rules are about structuring concepts – how you understand the world and classify things. That understanding is simply more basic than criteria for behavior. Common sense (and logic) dictates it.

So, if you want the behavioral rule ever to 'win' in this circumstance, the rule must shed its true self and somehow become an inference rule. Then it must be worked into the structure and logic of the decision table.

But do you really want to go there? Right now, the decision table is nice, neat, and easy to understand. Add in this 'exception' and the table becomes more complicated. Also, now you are literally 'programming' because you are creating a work-around for how rules operate naturally.

Consider these two additional real-life factors:

- How many other 'exceptions' might there be? You often find *quite* a few.
- How often do these 'exceptions' actually apply in ongoing activity? You often find they apply *only infrequently*.

So, your logic becomes skewed toward a great many edge cases seldom 'touched'. Complexity abounds. Not a good solution!

Possible Answer 2. The Behavioral Rule Should Win

Let's suppose the city wants the behavioral rule in this example to override the inference rules in the decision table (a much more likely scenario). The two-part solution is simple and logical. The second part is purely procedural. Note that this solution always works, even without a process model (though with a process model it becomes even easier.)

1. *Name things properly.* The outcome (conclusion) of the inference rules is re-named so that it can be distinguished from the outcome referenced by the behavioral rule. For example, the outcome of the inference rules above might be re-named *suggested recreational fee.*
2. *Process things properly.* The outcome referenced by the behavioral rule (*recreational* fee) is 'set' to the *suggested recreational fee* (the outcome referenced by the inference rules). If the 'set' operation fails due to the behavioral rule, then in effect the behavioral rule has overridden (*knocked-out*) the inference rules.

Remember, definitional rules (including inference rules) can never be broken. Their results have to be taken at face value. So, if an inference rule indicates the recreational fee has to be (say) $15 under a given set of conditions, then the recreation fee *has* to always be $15 in those conditions.

If there are circumstances where the recreational fee is *not* $15 in those conditions, then you simply have not said what you actually meant. You have named the outcome inaccurately or inappropriately. Perhaps you really meant *suggested* recreational fee (as above) or *normal* recreational fee.

In expressing rules, even with decision tables, you literally always need to say what you mean –and mean what you say.

Pre-Empting Inference Rules

A behavioral rule set up to pre-empt the result of some inference rules in special cases is so important that we give it a special name – *knock-out rule.*

> *A behavioral rule set up to pre-empt the result of some inference rules in special cases is called a knock-out rule.*

Aside: A behavioral rule could also be set up to 'knock out' the results of statistically-based decision logic (e.g., from machine learning models).

A knock-out rule excludes specific cases from 'normal' treatment as specified by the inference rules because the results might be unfair, unseemly, high-risk, or perverse. In the example above, the city wants to honor its senior citizens – not *penalize* them for exercising(!).

Knock-out rules are extremely common. For example, one of our clients in banking has very complex inference rules for assessing mortgage applications. Still, there are some basic knock-out rules. If you are underage or a felon, your application is never going to be approved, no matter what. Why should the decision logic ever even 'touch' those cases?!

In general, knock-out rules always should be evaluated before decision tables. It's just good practice. Where a step-by-step process model is in play, setting up that sequencing is straightforward. Then, violation of a knock-out rule should simply pre-empt the rules in the decision table from ever even being evaluated.

Postscript: The focus of this discussion is on decision tables because today that's where many or most professionals using current rule platforms encounter this kind of policy problem. Decision tables, however, are not the cause. The issue is with the platform being used. Any platform featuring inference rules, even apart from decision tables (e.g., old-style symbolic AI platforms), runs into the very same problem with policies (behavioral rules).

Part IV Summary

Rule Quality

A set of rules has high-quality if it is largely free of anomalies – irregularities, inconsistencies, conflicts, or misdirection. For the sake of all the non-developers in the world (which is most people) keep rules strictly disentangled from implementation code.

The worst possible time to find anomalies in rules is when people interact 'live' (including digitally). Anomalies in rules include:

- Conflicts
- Subsumptions
- Redundancies
- Incompleteness

High-quality rules are the lubricant that allows business and government to run smoothly and safely.

A true exception to a rule allows for a foreseen, explicit set of circumstances in which different-than-normal guidance is to be followed. Often what people see as an exception to a rule is not really an exception at all. This misperception can arise in several ways:

- Differential enforcement levels
- Special applicability conditions
- Knock-out rules for decision logic
- Advance authorizations

Decision tables are often rife with entries attempting to support 'exceptions', resulting in needless complexity. A behavioral rule set up to pre-empt the result of some inference rules (and reduce complexity among them) is called a *knock-out rule*.

The purpose of rules for communities and groups of people is first and foremost about communicating expectations for behavior, then enforcing those expectations. You should always be able to trust exactly what a rule statement says, so every rule statement should be *face-value trustworthy*. Clever 'hidden hands' to make rules work right might be acceptable in building bots to act intelligently, but bots aren't people.

Part V

Permissions, Authorizations, and Rights

When talking about rules for groups and communities of people, the scope is larger than you might imagine. For business and government, it also can (and almost certainly should) include permissions, authorizations, and rights. This part of the book explores these additional areas.

Do they seem foreign to rules? They shouldn't. They're just rules of different stripes.

Permissions, authorizations, and rights are just rules of different stripes.

Why is that insight so important? Besides the obvious fact that they too shape human activity and knowledge, there's another reason. By sharing the very same semantics as all other rules, bots can help ensure comprehensive logical consistency.

Imagine automated knowledge assistants helping us create guidance without deep flaws about very complex matters, then automating it directly without interpretation or much intervention by programmers. The opportunity is huge – maybe world-changing.

Honestly, we can't keep depending on software engineers to interpret and hand-code all this stuff in traditional programming languages. That's ultimately a dead end. Too time- and resource-consuming. Too error-prone in an increasingly risky world. It's time for a better approach.

We can't keep depending on software engineers to interpret and hand-code all this stuff in traditional programming languages. It's time for a better approach.

Terminology Adjustments

At this point, we need to make some adjustments in terminology. In the next chapter, we'll be discussing permissions – which by definition *aren't* rules per se. Then we need to talk about authorizations and rights, which introduce new wrinkles. Appendix I also discusses warranties. The full scope of guidance is actually goes well beyond rules alone.

So, instead of saying 'rules' now I'll often switch to the broader term 'elements of guidance'. When I need to refer to the full collection of elements of guidance, I'll often use the term 'body of guidance'.

Remember that *all* expressions for elements of guidance should be strictly declarative, including permissions, authorizations, and rights. The goal is a holistic guidance knowledgebase (rulebook) that can be evaluated automatically for consistency.

Chapter V-1

Permissions

Ever wish you could highlight what people are *allowed* to do as opposed to what they *must not?* A maze of prohibitions can be hard to navigate, especially for the uninitiated. Permissions offer a means to provide more positive and constructive guidance.

Consider the following statement:

Statement: *A person of any age is permitted to hold a bank account.*

This statement clearly gives guidance, possibly very useful, but it does not:

- Place any obligation or prohibition on business conduct. Therefore, it does not express a behavioral rule.
- Establish any necessity or impossibility for business knowledge. Therefore, it does not express a definitional rule.

In other words, the statement has removed no degree of freedom, so it's no rule at all. Yet the statement does talk factually about behavior. It does provide guidance – specifically about what is allowed. What is it then?

The statement expresses a *permission*. A permission specifically indicates consent for something. ('Something' in this discussion always specifically means 'some state of affairs'.) The supposition is that the something is not prohibited. Here's another example:

Payment-By-Cash Permission: *It is permitted that an order be paid by cash.*

This statement indicates that such behavior is allowed; in other words, that paying for an order by cash is not prohibited. The supposition is that there is (or should be) no rule to the contrary.

A permission specifically indicates consent for something.

Permission vs. Rule

Now consider this statement:

Permission: *An order $1,000 or less may be accepted on credit without a credit check.*

This statement also expresses a permission but it raises questions. Why does it specify the threshold '$1000'? Does some rule apply *above* that threshold? Perhaps the following rule?

Rule: *An order over $1,000 must not be accepted on credit without a credit check.*

Has that rule been captured? Is it valid?

Let's assume the rule has been captured and the business considers it valid. In that case, the rule is far more important than the permission. The rule removes a degree of freedom; the permission does not.

Now let's revisit the Payment-By-Cash Permission from earlier.

Payment-By-Cash Permission: *It is permitted that an order be paid by cash.*

This permission also raises questions. Why does it single out 'cash'? Do some rule(s) apply to other forms of payment, for example by promissory note? Let's say such a rule does exist.

IOU Rule: *An order must not be paid by a promissory note.*

This rule indicates that workers are not free to accept IOUs for payment of orders. That particular degree of freedom has been removed or diminished. Depending on enforcement level, violating the rule invites response, which might be anything from outright rejection and/or severe sanction, to mild tutelage.

Again, let's assume the business needs the IOU Rule and considers it valid. As before, the rule is far more important than the permission. The rule removes a degree of freedom; the permission does not.

A rule removes a degree of freedom; a permission does not.

Note that other degrees of freedom have *not* been removed or diminished by the IOU Rule. For example, unless other rules pertain to how orders are paid, workers are free to accept cash. In the sense that the IOU Rule doesn't expressly prohibit payment by cash, such permission is already implicit. Strictly speaking, the Payment-By-Cash Permission isn't needed.

Retaining Explicit Permissions

Since permission is always implicit where there are no rules, is expressing and retaining permissions ever useful? *Sometimes.* Consider the earlier Bank Account Permission:

Bank Account Permission: *A person of any age is permitted to hold a bank account.*

Suppose this permission reflects the final resolution of a long-standing debate in the business about how old a person must be to hold a bank account. Some say 21, others 18, some 12, and some say there should be no age restriction at all. Finally, the issue is resolved in favor of no age restriction – there's no rule about that. Here, the absence of a rule is definitely worth recording!

In this way, permissions can serve as an element of corporate memory about resolutions to policy questions in favor of *no rule*.

Permissions can serve as an element of corporate memory about resolutions to policy questions in favor of no rule.

Other reasons for including permissions in a body of guidance include:

- To inform or re-assure parties that some specific degree of freedom does exist.
- To provide a basis for admonishing workers about applying some rule that does not actually exist.
- To guide the crafting of guidance messages for rules. (Refer to Chapter III-3.) A guidance message can even *be* a formally-stated permission. For example, the Payment-By-Cash Permission can be a guidance message for the IOU Rule.

Expressing Permissions

For permission statements to serve a formal purpose, they need to be expressed following all the basic guidelines discussed in Part II for rules. (Otherwise, they are just instructions or informal guidance messages.) Once good habits are developed for expressing rules, well-expressed permissions follow naturally.

In particular, permissions should strictly adhere to the same concept model (as expressed by a structured business vocabulary) as rules. In holistic treatment of guidance all elements need to be based on common semantics so the whole guidance knowledgebase (rulebook) can be disambiguated and de-conflicted at scale.

Like rules, explicit permissions should always be *face-value trustworthy*. One implication is that no assumptions are to be made about issues of guidance that the permission doesn't address explicitly. Consider the permission from earlier:

Permission: *An order $1,000 or less may be accepted on credit without a credit check.*

This permission makes no assertion about the range above the $1,000 threshold. Just because the permission says an order $1,000 or less may be accepted on credit without a credit check, that does not necessarily mean an order over $1,000 *must not*. Like rules and all declarative guidance, a permission only says just what it says.

Like rules, a permission only says just what it says.

Conflicts Among Rules and Permissions

Another implication of explicit permissions being *face-value trustworthy* is that they must not conflict with any rules involving prohibitions. For example, suppose your body of guidance includes both the following statements:

Permission: *It is permitted that an order be paid by cash.*

Prohibition: *A phone order must not be paid by cash.*

These elements of guidance are in direct conflict. Conflicts must be resolved. Assuming the rule is valid, the simplest solution is to drop (discontinue or exclude) the permission. Or the permission can be revised as follows:

Permission: *It is permitted that an order be paid by cash <u>if the order is not by phone.</u>*

Aside: An additional solution to this general problem is presented in Chapter V-3. For more about conflicts between modalities, refer to Appendix F.

On the other hand, suppose the original permission is valid. In that case, the rule should be dropped (discontinued or excluded).

Conflicts between permissions and rules aren't always so obvious. For example, suppose a restaurant posts the following sign:

Sign: *Gratuities appreciated, but no tips please.*

As discussed in Chapter IV-2, whether this statement contradicts itself is entirely bound up in the definitional criteria for 'tip' and 'gratuity' (that devil in the definitional details!). Let's suppose that gratuities and tips *do* represent the same concept. Let's also reword the statement a bit more directly:

Statement: *Gratuities permitted. Tips prohibited.*

Clearly a conflict. Something has to give!

The ambiguity of the original sign might be intentional, of course, as a fun message (prompt?) to customers. In that case, the message doesn't need to be included in the body of guidance at all.

Permission vs. Guideline/Suggestion

A permission is not the same as a guideline or suggestion. How do they differ?

- A permission expresses that no constraint applies to something. Because no constraint is applied, a permission can never be violated. It is a consent, not an entitlement. (See Chapter V-3 on rights.) Consequently, permissions never have any enforcement level or violation responses. They simply acknowledge that something is allowed.

Aside: Since a permission has flash points just like rules, acknowledgements of permitted behavior could be presented to actors in real-time. The justification for interrupting ongoing work, however, would have to be strong. Nonetheless, such acknowledgements might play a role in positive reinforcement, especially during training. (Refer to Appendix G.)

- In contrast to a permission, a guideline or suggestion communicates a different way (hopefully in real time) in which something can be done or accomplished. It hints that some behavior might be nonstandard, suboptimal, or deprecated. Since a guideline or suggestion can be violated, it is a behavioral rule, even if such violation serves simply as an opportunity for tutoring. Like any behavioral rule, a guideline or suggestion has an enforcement level (the very thing that makes it a guideline or suggestion). It also potentially has some violation response(s).

A permission is consent,
not a guideline or suggestion.

Onward!

At this point you might be viewing permissions as always more or less gentle elements of guidance. Unlike rules, they remove no degree of freedom.

Wait, not so fast! Don't think for a second that we've exhausted the potential of permissions. In fact, we've just begun. Permissions are fundamental to setting up authorizations, which can be accomplished in a surprisingly simple and straightforward way. Read on to the next chapter!

Chapter V-2

Authorizations

Those are pianos under the covers in the picture. The signs are on top of them. Pretty ironic, wouldn't you say? Can you figure out how the signs could have ended up there without somebody having violated a rule? The (simple) solution is given at the end of this chapter.

Permissions and Prohibitions

A beautiful university I visit regularly has a sign posted near its arched walkways:

> University Rule: *No photography without permission.*

(I'd show you a picture of it, but I wasn't authorized.)

The university sign expresses very interesting guidance. It prohibits something (photography at that place), but allows the prohibition to be overcome with explicit permission. ('Something' in this discussion always specifically means 'some state of affairs'.)

More precisely, the prohibition can be overcome *only* by explicit permission. That's not how prohibitions normally work. Generally, prohibitions apply to everyone without exception. What's going on? To understand, we need to dig deeper into basic assumptions about rules.

Optimistic World vs. Pessimistic World

The default assumption about rules can be called an *optimistic world*.

Optimistic World: *Anything is permitted unless expressly prohibited.*

The default assumption about rules is an optimistic world: Anything is permitted unless expressly prohibited.

In other words, no prohibitions apply to anything until expressed explicitly. Degrees of freedom are removed consciously and selectively. Freedom to act is not granted or awarded; it simply exists a priori.

An optimistic world is essentially one that assumes the best from everybody. That world view aligns comfortably with promoting creativity and innovation. Rules are introduced only where sound motivation exists for them (e.g., protecting against significant risks, ensuring fidelity of service, supporting data quality, etc.).

An optimistic world, of course, is not prudent concerning use of, and/or access to, resources that are deemed especially sensitive, dangerous, scarce, privileged, and/or valuable. Think of your bank accounts, digital devices, and social media accounts, for example.

For that reason, it makes sense to grant permission for their use and/or access on a selective, deliberate basis. This is the world of security, special privileges, and authorizations – a pessimistic world where actors are selectively authorized to do certain things.

> Pessimistic World: *Everything is prohibited unless expressly permitted.*

Needing to selectively authorize actors to do things represents a pessimistic world: Everything is prohibited unless expressly permitted.

Unlike the optimistic world, which requires no overt specification, a pessimistic world must be declared explicitly.

Doing so is not hard though. The University Rule, in fact, did just that. After looking into the matter, I found that the university required photographers to register, and schedule a certain date and time to take photographs around the arches. They literally give out authorizations in advance. (I even learned the motivation – too many professional photographers blocking the archways with too much equipment in the late evening hours.)

Exclusion Zones and Authorizations

Authorizations require setting up an exclusion zone in which something is prohibited unless expressly authorized (i.e., creating a selective pessimistic world). Ever see a sign posted on a door that said *Authorized Personnel Only?* That door is *literally* the entrance to an exclusion zone.

Just like the door sign, the University Rule sign set up its exclusion zone by physical context – the sign was posted right in front of the arches. Unfortunately, assuming context always invites ambiguity. For example, how far did the university's exclusion zone actually extend? Only around those arches? To other arches as well? The whole university? For formal authorizations, exclusion zones must be specified carefully.

Consider another example. A company naturally wants to control who makes payments from its financial resources, so it specifies the following exclusion zone:

> Payments Exclusion Zone: *A person is permitted to make a payment from the company's accounts only if the person is authorized explicitly.*

> *Aside:* Although expressed as a restricted permission statement ('... is permitted ... only if'), the rule establishes a prohibition. Refer to Appendix M.

This rule sets up an exclusion zone on making payments from the company's accounts. Doing so requires a person to be specifically authorized. Persons not explicitly authorized are not permitted to do so.

How can people be authorized to make payments? The trick is viewing permissions in a new and different light. In a pessimistic world, permissions assume a new role – now they are *authorizations*. Here are some examples for the Payments Exclusion Zone.

> Authorization: *Jane Smith is permitted to make a payment from the company's accounts.*

> Authorization: *Any senior manager is permitted to make a payment from the company's accounts.*

The first authorization stipulates that a specific person (Jane Smith) may make payments. The second authorization is role-based – a blanket permission that allows any person who is a senior manager to make payments.

Remember: *The important thing about all these examples is not the specific syntax used to express them, but rather to illustrate how authorizations fit neatly with other forms of guidance. The goal is a holistic guidance knowledgebase (rulebook) that can be evaluated for logical consistency by bots.*

Now 'authorization' can be defined more precisely. An authorization is an explicit permission by some authority that gives validity to the acts of some persons or agents that otherwise would be prohibited.

An authorization is an explicit permission by some authority that gives validity to the acts of some persons or agents that otherwise would be prohibited.

Authorizations are not rules per se. They are permissions. However, authorizations are always logically linked to some rule – the one that establishes the underlying exclusion zone.

Specifying Authorizations

Like rules, authorizations need to be deconflicted and unambiguous with respect to all other guidance. Therefore, specification of authorizations should be based on the same semantics (structured business vocabulary) as all rules. Here is another example:

Exclusion Zone: *A vehicle may use an ice road only if the use is authorized explicitly.*

In this example, the risky resource is 'ice roads'. The authority that created this prohibition is pessimistic about the safety of ice roads and wants to coordinate their use carefully.

Here is an authorization that permits some usage:

Authorization: *An ice road north of the Arctic Circle may be used by any vehicle.*

This authorization permits any ice road above the Arctic Circle to be used by any vehicle, presumably because those ice roads stay frozen year-round. (Let's do hope that assumption is true – and continues to prove so in the future!)

Tables can also be used to specify authorizations. For example:

Exclusion Zone: *A party may pull a permit only if the license they hold explicitly authorizes that type of permit.*

Authorization Table

✓ - authorized

		Permit Type						
		Residential Addition	Residential Baby Barrier	Residential Boatlift	Residential Pool or Spa	Residential Roof	Residential Generator	etc.
License Held	Owner-Builder	✓	✓	✓	✓	✓	✓	
	Certified Building	✓	✓	✓				
	Certified General	✓	✓	✓	✓	✓		
	Certified Residential	✓	✓	✓			✓	
	Registered Building	✓	✓	✓				
	Registered General	✓	✓	✓		✓	✓	
	Certified Marine			✓				
	Registered Swimming Pool Class A		✓		✓			
	Local Fence		✓					
	Registered Roofing					✓		
	Certified Master Electrician						✓	
	Certified Master Plumber						✓	
	etc.							

Aside: This authorization table is not a decision table. No logical implications are involved.

Authorizations vs. Violation Responses

If a person or agent is authorized to do something within an exclusion zone, then no violation occurs when they do that something. An authorization is not some kind of violation response. A violation response can occur only if an attempted or actual violation of a rule occurs.

For behavioral rules with tolerant enforcement levels, violations can still be overcome. An obvious case is under the enforcement level 'guideline'. Another is under the enforcement level 'override with real-time waiver'. (Refer to Appendix H.) Overcoming a violation, however, is not at all the same as no violation whatsoever having happened.

One implication, perhaps obvious, is that authorizations must be specified *prior* to the prohibited behavior taking place. In other words, authorizations must be specified *before* application of relevant guidance (rules) for some behavior (flash point). An authorization is deliberate *advance* permission, not some special form of real-time dispensation.

An authorization is deliberate advance permission, not some special form of real-time dispensation.

Summary: Permissions with Teeth

The difference between a normal permission and an authorization is that with a normal permission you can still do something even without the permission unless there is some rule against it. It's an optimistic world. Everything is permitted unless explicitly prohibited. In that world, the rules rule.

Authorizations, in contrast, represent a pessimistic world. Nobody can do something unless explicitly permitted. A rule sets up an exclusion zone that disallows doing the something without an explicit authorization. Permissions become mandatory. Within an exclusion zone, the authorizations 'rule'.

A world where permissions have teeth is literally a very different world. So too is the world of rights, as the next chapter explains.

Solution for the Piano Signs

Exclusion Zone: *An object may be placed on a piano only if authorized explicitly.*

Authorization: *A sign is permitted on a piano indicating nothing should be placed on the piano.*

Authorization: *A protective covering over a piano is permitted.*

Did you catch the need for the second authorization?

Chapter V-3

Rights

Consider the Commandment *Thou shalt not kill.* The Commandment places an obligation on all members of the community not to kill. How does the Commandment apply to me personally? First, since I'm obviously a member of the community, I must not kill.

The Commandment also applies to me in a second way, less obvious, but equally important. It confers a *right* to me – my right *not to be* killed by a member of the community. In groups and communities of people, obligations and prohibitions always establish rights, even if never articulated.

In groups and communities of people, obligations and prohibitions always establish rights.

A right can be viewed as an entitlement. Suppose a city has the following rule.

Senior Citizen Rule: *A senior citizen must be allowed use of the city's recreational facilities whenever open.*

This rule establishes a right, an entitlement, which might be expressed as follows. (As for all examples, the specific syntax is not particularly important for this discussion.)

Senior Citizen Right: *A senior citizen is not to be denied use of the city's recreational facilities whenever open.*

Behavioral rules and rights come in pairs. Where there's a behavioral rule, there's a right.

Behavioral rules and rights come in pairs. Where there's a behavioral rule, there's a right.

Aside: Rights, of course, should not conflict with other rules (and rights). For additional discussion, see Appendix B.

Sometimes, rights are better known and more visible than the paired rule. This is often the case in law and contracts.

First Amendment Right. The First Amendment in the Bill of Rights of the U.S. Constitution declares freedom of speech as a fundamental right of the people in the community. For the sake of simplicity, the right might be worded as follows:

First Amendment Right: *A person is entitled to freedom of speech.*

Even so, there is an implicit rule:

Rule: *A person must not be denied freedom of speech.*

Fifth Amendment Right. The Fifth Amendment of the U.S. Constitution protects a person from being compelled to self-incriminate. So, protection against forced self-incrimination is also a fundamental right. For simplicity, this right might be worded as follows:

Fifth Amendment Right: *A person need not self-incriminate.*

Again, there is an implicit rule:

Rule: *A person must not be required to self-incriminate.*

Rights and Definitions

As always there is no escaping definitions.

First Amendment Right. What does the term 'freedom of speech' mean? Are you free to shout "Fire!" in a crowded theater just for kicks? No. That cannot be considered a case (instance) of freedom of speech.

I'm not a lawyer and I haven't studied the relevant case law for freedom of speech. But I'm sure the rule about not shouting 'Fire!' in crowded theaters for kicks is not the only limitation on freedom of speech. The definition is no doubt complex, and the number of definitional rules extensive.

What do those definitional criteria do? As discussed in Chapter I-5, they determine whether or not any particular case is an instance of the concept. (Here, a case is someone speaking, and the concept is freedom of speech.)

Could all those rules be automated? I don't know. Up to a point, perhaps. (Personally, if I were a defendant in a court case, I'd still want humans in the loop.)

Fifth Amendment Right. The term 'self-incrimination' is loaded with meaning and the relevant case law again extensive. Being forced to testify in a court case against yourself is an obvious example. But what about other circumstances? How about a blood or DNA sample taken by police without your consent? Can that be a case of self-incrimination? As always, first and foremost are definitions and definitional rules.

Right vs. Permission

A permission indicates explicit consent that something is allowed for a community or group of people. ('Something' in this discussion always specifically means 'some state of affairs'.) Consent, however, is not at all the same thing as a right. Mere consent is not entitlement.

A permission is not a right. Mere consent is not entitlement.

Example 1. Consider the permission discussed in Chapter V-1:

Permission: *A person of any age is permitted to hold a bank account.*

The bank might have rules that prevent some people from holding a bank account.

Rule: *A person convicted of financial fraud must not hold a bank account.*

For any person convicted of financial fraud, the rule 'wins' over the permission. Consent is not entitlement.

Example 2. Consider the following permission.

Permission: *An employee is permitted to enter a company building.*

Obviously, not all employees in every circumstance are permitted to enter every company building all the time. Consider the following rules:

Rule: *An employee may enter a company building only if the employee holds a valid company id on their person when they enter.*

Rule: *An employee may enter a hazardous materials test facility only if explicitly authorized.*

Rule: *A person may enter a building on fire only if the person is a credentialed first responder.*

All these rules 'win' over the permission. An employee is not entitled to enter all company buildings all the time, rather only as the rules permit. Mere consent is not entitlement.

The permission as expressed above is not face-value trustworthy (see Chapter V-1) and is therefore defective. At least three rules (as listed) contradict it in certain situations. If retained, it should be expressed as simply a policy – i.e., as an element of guidance that is not practicable (see Chapter II-1).

Building Entry Policy: *In general, an employee may enter a company building.*

Precisely. *In general* – but *only* in general – the policy holds true. The real question is when does it *not* hold true. The rules answer that.

Declaring Rights

Do all rights need to be explicitly acknowledged? Not necessarily. Consider the following example.

Rule: *No swimming in this pond at any time.*

Is there a corresponding right? Yes.

Right: *You can expect this pond to be swimmer-less at all times.*

Is it important to explicitly acknowledge this right? Probably not. (But don't forget it's there!)

Is it important to explicitly acknowledge all rights? Probably not. But don't forget they're there!

Are there circumstances in which the right might be preferred over the rule? Yes, sometimes rules are expressed that might work better as rights. Here's an example from Chapter IV-1.

Gold Customer Access Rule: *A gold customer must be allowed access to the warehouse at all hours.*

A right for gold customers, of course, is implicit in the rule. Their entitlement could be expressed as follows.

Warehouse Access Right: *A gold customer can access the warehouse at all hours.*

The counterpart in Chapter IV-1 of the rule above was:

General Access Rule: *A customer that is not a gold customer may have access to the warehouse only during regular business hours.*

Now, assuming the Right is explicit, that rule can be restated as follows:

General Access Rule: *A customer without the Warehouse Access Right may have access to the warehouse only during regular business hours.*

As this rewording illustrates, rights can be referenced by rules. An advantage is to insulate the referencing rule (in this case, the General Access Rule) from changes to the Right. For example, in the future silver customers might gain the right to access the warehouse at all hours. 'Silver customer' need be added only in the expression of the Right.

Rights and Contracts

Quite possibly, the Warehouse Access Right might be part of an explicit arrangement an organization has signed with a gold customer. Such rights are common in contracts and agreements between parties.

"A contract right flows from another party's duty to perform ... The person to whom the performance is owed has a right to that performance. Therefore, if there is a duty, there is a correlative right."[26]

'Duty' in this context implies obligation (i.e., a rule).

What does a right included in a contract or agreement mean in the larger context of rules? In addition to enforcement of the associated rule, it means two things:

[26] Drafting Contracts: *How and Why Lawyers Do What They Do*, Tina L. Stark, Wolters Kluwer, Aspen Publishers, 2007, pp. 23-24.

1. *Within the scope of the draft document.* The parties agree not to revise or amend the document to contradict any given right (unless deleted or revised). Imagine live digital contracts where the parties can amend contracts more directly. Rights included therein put a brake on thwarting or undermining original intent.
2. *Within subsequent business activity.* Assuming the parties are good citizens, they both must introduce the rights into their own individual spheres of operations – more specifically, into each of their own (larger) bodies of guidance. By at least the time of contract activation (but hopefully before), conflicts between the rights specified in the agreement and their own existing rules must be discovered and resolved.

Consider how poor most organizations are today about undertaking the latter responsibility on a day-to-day basis. The task is labor-intensive and often hit-or-miss. Want to meet stakeholder expectations? Smarten up your ability to digitally absorb the rights and rules in contracts!

Want to meet stakeholder expectations?
Smarten up your ability to absorb contracts!

Part V Summary

Permissions, Authorizations, and Rights

Permissions, authorizations, and rights shouldn't seem foreign to rules. They're just rules of different stripes.

- A *permission* specifically indicates consent for something. The supposition is that the something is not prohibited. Unlike a rule, a permission does not remove any degree of freedom. Permissions can serve as an element of corporate memory about resolutions to policy questions in favor of *no rule*.
- An *authorization* is an explicit permission by some authority that gives validity to the acts of some persons or agents that otherwise would be prohibited. An authorization is deliberate advance permission, not some special form of real-time dispensation.
- A *right* reflects an entitlement to something. In groups and communities of people, for every rule there is a right, even if not expressed explicitly. Rights are especially important in law and contracts.

We can't keep coding guidance of all these kinds in programming languages. It's ultimately a dead end.

The concept model diagram in Figure 1 illustrates the structural connections between the various kinds of elements of guidance. Relevant definitions are found in the Glossary. Discussion of warranties is presented in Appendix P. In the diagram:

- Noun concepts are indicated using boxes labeled by terms.

- Heavy dark lines indicate categories.
- Verb concepts are indicated using worded lines and arrows.

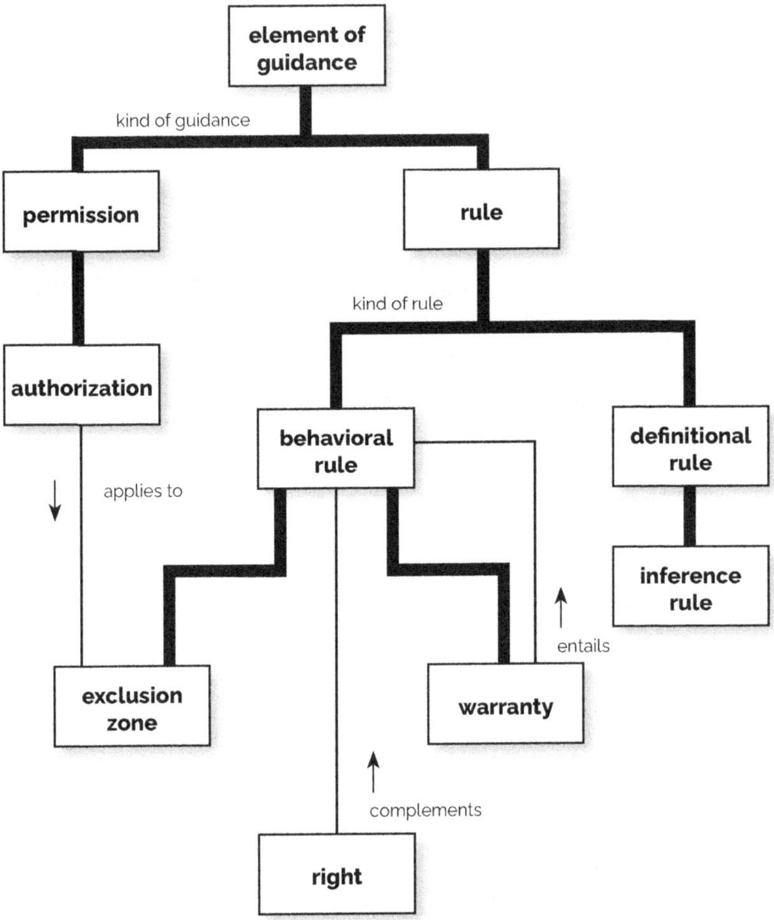

Figure 1. *Structural Connections Between the Various Kinds of Elements of Guidance*

A body of guidance can include all the elements of guidance in Figure 1, plus definitions and policies. The real scope of rules (and 'rulebook') goes well beyond rules alone.

Conclusion

Rule Platforms in Business & Government

The opportunity for rule platforms in the coming years is to get smarter about the fundamental needs of groups and communities of *people*. These needs include:

- Better governance.
- Digital absorption of laws, regulations, contracts, and agreements.
- Smart touch points that today's digital systems often lack.
- Diminished programmer workload. (Refer to Appendix P.)

Essential in that regard is recognizing that many rules can be violated. It's so obvious. It's a mystery why, two decades into the 21st century, rule platforms don't directly support behavioral rules. Selective responses to violations of behavioral rules allow *real-time:*

- Insertion of human discretion, sentiment, and common sense into ongoing activities.
- Pinpoint dissemination of needed knowledge.
- Prevention of data defects.

Not catching attempted violations of behavioral rules in real time causes snowballing errors downstream and thus extensive rework. No wonder data quality remains so bad and business software so complex and brittle. That work is currently being left to software developers – and their skills and incentives simply don't align very well with it.

Business and government need platforms such that people (not just software engineers) can work directly with behavioral and definitional rules. The platform should assist people with disambiguation, refinement, verification, implementation, and management of the rules. Work within the platform should be visible and traceable all the way from the initial drafting of policies through to automated application.

The opportunity for rule platforms in the coming years is to get smarter about the fundamental needs of groups and communities of people.

Natural Language

A key factor in considering how rule platforms could better support business and government is to remember how guidance is formally communicated. It's expressed in *natural language* in documents, starting with policies and directives.

On top of that is an array of legal documents, almost all pure text as well, including:

- laws
- acts
- statutes
- regulations
- contracts
- agreements
- MOUs
- deals
- leases
- licenses
- certifications
- deeds
- warranties
- legal notices
- etc.

Alongside these are authoritative sources of science and engineering knowledge, documents which are also often extensively framed in text.

Like it or not, policy makers and knowledge workers by and large will never learn a different means to represent, revise, or disambiguate the policies, rules, and other content already expressed in these artifacts. And why should they?!

Yet most rule platforms today don't support any form of natural language. How well do you think a rule platform will fare among policy professionals, business people, and knowledge workers without such support?![27]

Unfortunately, most rule platforms to date have assiduously avoided natural language in any form, as well as its natural cohort, business semantics. They were simply not originally developed to address the problem of organizing and documenting rules for groups and communities of people.

> *Aside:* Most existing rule platforms were originally created to emulate human intelligence (e.g., expert systems) and/or to support architectural separation at runtime between business content that changes frequently and other programming code.

In general, rule platforms have not come to grips with the fact that rules for groups and communities of people are first and foremost a communication problem, *not* an engineering problem. Also, the industry seems to have a fixation on perfect disambiguation (impossible), rather than on pragmatic disambiguation beyond a reasonable doubt in a well-defined context. (Refer to Chapter II-5.)

It would be hugely productive to reach a pragmatic middle ground where humans contribute structured business vocabularies based on concept models, and machines exploit those specifications to assist with automated disambiguation of rule statements in some form of controlled natural language. Yes, it's a hard problem – but by no means is it impossible.

In the day and age of machine learning (ML) and statistical AI, a language-based (symbolic) approach for rules might seem out of touch. *No!* It's not old-fashioned and it's never actually been solved.

---

[27] Oracle Intelligent Advisor (formerly Oracle Policy Automation (OPA)) was an early pioneer and exception in this regard.

In a day and age when you can Google almost anything, it's amazing in fact that it hasn't already happened. We need to envision a new partnership between humans and machines, one more directly suitable to governance.

We need to envision a new partnership between humans and machines, one more directly suitable to governance.

Closing the Governance Gap

Lack of support for some form of natural language leaves a huge gap right at the heart of organizations. And it's not just a technological gap, it's also a *traceability* gap. Why?

Today, automating governance sources requires *translation*, not just interpretation. Under the very best of circumstances, this translation is into specific parameter settings for some automated tool(s). Far more common is translation into procedural coding languages – a.k.a. *programming*.

Indeed, the overwhelming majority of rules for business and government is still implemented using procedural software languages not at all built for that purpose. That simply won't do.

The overwhelming majority of rules for business and government are still implemented using procedural software languages not at all built for that purpose.

The resulting gap from a governance perspective is illustrated in Figure 1.

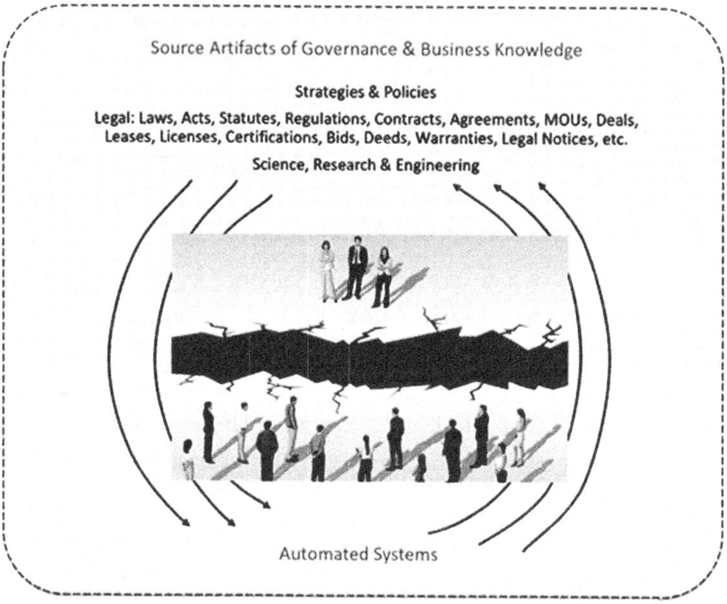

Figure 1. *The Governance Gap*

What impacts does the gap have for the day-to-day needs and practices of business and government?

- *Loss of traceability.* Top-down, it's hard to determine what pieces of code implement which policy so as to prove that obligations have been met correctly. Compliance professionals feel this pain acutely (or sometimes are simply too numb to articulate it).

  Loss of traceability, however, works both ways. Bottom-up, it's hard to determine real-life motivation for crucial pieces of code so as to understand what results should be considered authentic.

  So, impact assessment is difficult and time-consuming in *both* directions. Nobody enjoys it or feels very productive doing it.

- *Diminished agility.* Change is far harder than it needs to be. It's not possible simply to re-state and re-interpret the content of source artifacts through to implementation, watching for conflicts, gaps, and inconsistencies – including, of course, inter-artifact clashes. That's hard enough on its own. Instead, change almost always requires programmer intervention.

  That software work, in turn, is not simply a matter of translating modifications into computer code. First, developers must do fine-grained detective work to determine what code needs to be revised or replaced where, work that is often very time-consuming and error-prone in its own regard. It's not a happy overall mix whatsoever!

- *Poor corporate memory.* In an ever more fluid digital workplace, who can possibly remember that some new bit of code implemented some revised piece of policy in a particular way for a given reason?!

  Rules for groups and communities of people always pertain to corporate memory. (Perhaps we should call *it community* memory instead!) In this regard, it is no surprise that the law is so relevant to the discussion in this book. With regard to everyday business activity, does the following sound familiar?[28]

  "One of the important roles of a contract is memory, in at least two different ways: 1. The recollections and expectations of the original parties diverge with time. 2. In business life, the original definers of the deal, and hence of the contract, move on and are replaced by people who do not know the deal except from the written documentation."

---

[28] *Contract Drafting to Software Specification: Linguistic Sources of Ambiguity: A Handbook*, Version 1.0, November 2003, by Daniel M. Berry, Ph.D., Erik Kamsties, Ph.D., and Michael M. Krieger, Ph.D., J.D., p. 17.

Policy and knowledge are never static. Unforeseen events (e.g., pandemics) *will* happen. Hard-coded, long-forgotten policies and rules embedded in legacy *will* have knock-on effects as new policies and rules are introduced. The problem is not about speed of software deployment per se; it's about having a governance mechanism to evaluate new circumstances comprehensively and react appropriately.

Creating and deploying policy and rules into day-to-day business operations is at the very heart of business governance. Such creation and deployment should be:

- timely
- effective
- selective
- pervasive
- traceable
- transparent
- repeatable
- retractable

Does the need for such policy-oriented rule platforms seem obvious? *Yes, it is!* Being rule-based is the most basic characteristic of Western civilization. We need to do it better!

Being rule-based is the most basic characteristic of Western civilization. We need to do it better!

Appendix A

Concept Model Diagram for Factual Expression of Rules

The concept model diagram in Figure 1 illustrates the core concepts and structural relationships for supporting factual expression of rules. Relevant definitions are found in the Glossary. In the diagram:

- Noun concepts are indicated using boxes labeled by terms.
- Heavy dark lines indicate categories.
- Verb concepts are indicated using worded lines and arrows.

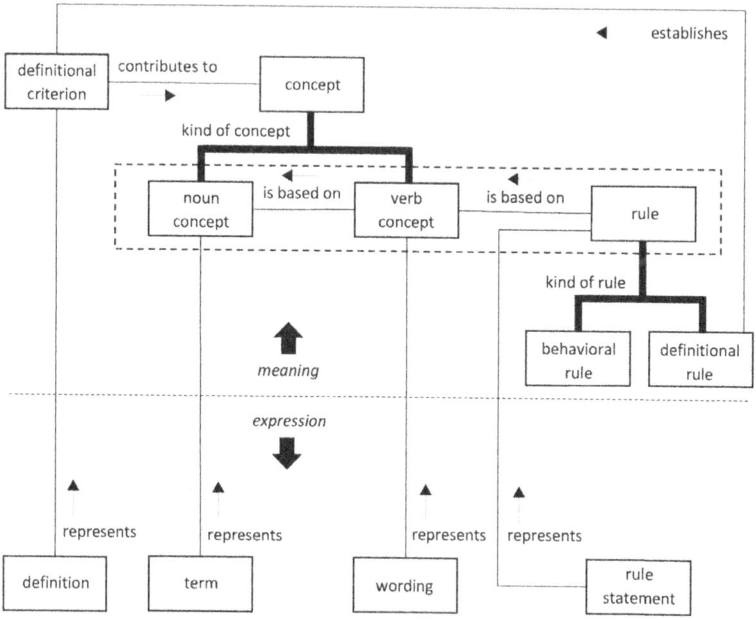

Figure 1. *Concept Model Diagram for Factual Expression of Rules*

Key observations:

- The dashed-line box in middle of the diagram (reading from right to left) calls out the core notion that rules (and all other kinds of declarative statements) are based on verb concepts, and verb concepts, in turn, are based on noun concepts.
- The boxes and structure in the top of the diagram are about pure meaning. The boxes in the bottom of the diagram are about communicating meanings. This distinction is essential for support of multi-language and synonymous expressions of all kinds. The implication for rules is that an expression of a rule is not the rule; the *meaning* of the rule is the rule.
- A concept is formed by definitional criteria (top left of the diagram), which can arise from either definitions or definitional rules, or both. One implication is that all concepts could be formed by definitional rules alone, although not recommended in practice.

Aside: This concept model diagram presents a *highly* simplified version of the OMG specification SBVR *(Semantics of Business Vocabulary and Business Rules).*

Appendix B

Ensuring Logical Consistency of Guidance

All elements of guidance should share both the same business semantics (concept model expressed by a structured business vocabulary) and logical foundations. By specifying all guidance on a common base, bots can help ensure logical consistency.[29] It's the only scalable way to de-conflict and disambiguate bodies of guidance of any significant size.

Rules vs. Actions

Maintaining the distinction between rules and actions is critical. Restricting rules to states of affairs creates a guidance knowledgebase (rulebook) with clear boundaries within which consistency and correctness can be verified automatically based on logic. Invoking actions can have unknown consequences (aka side effects) for that knowledgebase. Strict separation of concerns is essential. (One consequence is that violation responses are not considered part of behavioral rules per se.)

Many current rule platforms allow 'rules' to invoke actions. Mixed with any number of inference rules in some application logic (e.g., an expert system), such support not only causes huge (and unnecessary) complexity, but also virtually guarantees the logic is inaccessible for business people.

---

[29] Refer to *Business Knowledge Messaging: How to Avoid Business Miscommunication*, by Ronald G. Ross, 2022, Chapter 8.

Activation vs. Application of Guidance

The worst possible time to discover anomalies and ambiguity is when some element(s) of guidance are actually applied. At the very least, your business partners might see your dirty laundry. Worst is they proceed to exploit it – or take you to court. Understanding the distinction between activation of guidance vs. application of guidance is therefore essential.

- *Application of guidance* is when some element(s) of guidance are applied (used) to evaluate a set of circumstances in actually operating the business (hopefully in real time and in automated fashion). That set of circumstances might necessitate evaluating some behavior (e.g., a customer making a purchase) or making an operational business decision (e.g., which up-sell or cross-sell product(s) to suggest to the customer).
- *Activation of guidance* is any point in time when some element(s) of guidance is/are officially made part of the in-practice (live) body of guidance. It's at this point in time when the entire guidance knowledgebase (rulebook) should be free of conflicts and ambiguity, so the guidance is 'clean' before actually being applied (used). (It makes no difference whether or not the element(s) of guidance is/are automatable.)

Note carefully that rules are 'live' (ready to be evaluated) from the point of their individual or group activation. Actual evaluation does not happen, however, until some related flash point occurs, decision is requested, calculation result is needed, etc.

Aside: The discussion in Chapter IV-3 of knock-out rules (how a behavioral rule can 'win' over inference rules) assumed time of application, *not* time of activation. Discovery of potential clashes could (and probably should), however, take place at time of activation.

Elements of guidance can exist in draft form before activation, of course, and can even be assessed for anomalies and ambiguities. But the time of activation is an important gateway into the business bloodstream – one essential for good governance.

Discovering Anomalies in Guidance

Consider the following example (extended from Chapter V-3). Suppose a city wants to establish the following right. (As for all examples, the specific syntax is not particularly important for this discussion.)

Senior Citizen Right: *A senior citizen is not to be denied use of the city's recreational facilities whenever open.*

Specifying this right has the following effects:

- *At the time of the right's activation.* The body of guidance is checked for conflicts. These conflicts must be resolved. Suppose the following prohibition is currently in effect:

  Saturday Rule: *A senior citizen is not permitted use of open recreational facilities of the city on Saturdays.*

  This rule is in conflict with the new right. For the new right to be activated, the Saturday Rule must be revoked (deactivated).

- *After the time of the right's activation.* The right's role is as a sentinel against any new or revised rule that conflicts with the right. For example, suppose an attempt is made to introduce (activate) the following new prohibition:

  Sunday Rule: *A senior citizen is not permitted use of open recreational facilities of the city <u>on Sundays</u>.*

  This new rule conflicts with the right. For the Sunday Rule to be activated, the existing right would have to be revoked (deactivated).

Automated Consistency Checking

Anomalies can easily occur among the rules found in decision tables. Fortunately, automated tools have been available in that context for many years to help detect and avoid many such problems. The uniformity of decision tables, a characteristic not shared by behavioral rules and related definitional rules, makes such automated support relatively straightforward.

Sadly, such tools do not, however, address semantic issues. For example, assessing the completeness of a decision table is based simply on every possible combination of values for the considerations. Such structural 'completeness' can be something of a mirage.

As of this writing, nothing equivalent exists for behavioral rules and related definitional rules. It is hardly surprising such tools do not exist; there is no purely structural pattern (such as a table) to exploit for them. Discovering anomalies will have to be done either by brute computing force (as in machine learning), a semantic approach to natural language processing (NLP), or (more likely) some combination of both.

A distinction that arose in expert systems will continue to prove useful for the future:

- *Validation:* ensuring the correctness of some rule(s) with respect to business or community purpose
- *Verification:* assessing the fitness of some rule(s) with respect to logical consistency; looking for anomalies in (some) rule(s) (usually two or more in combination)

With respect to rules for groups and communities of people, even when tooling arrives to address the latter, the former will remain a crucial task for humans.

Appendix C

About Decision Tables

Decision tables are a convenient format for expressing and managing inference rules aimed at making the same kind of operational business decision using the same set of conditions (or subsets thereof), but for different facts (think 'data').

For example, these three inference rules make the same kind of operational business decision (preference level of customer) using the same set of conditions:

> Platinum Customer Rule: *A customer is considered a platinum customer if the customer places at least 48 large orders during a two-calendar-year period that are each fully paid within 45 days.*
>
> Gold Customer Rule: *A customer is considered a gold customer if the customer places 12-47 large orders during a one-calendar-year period that are each fully paid within 60 days.*
>
> Silver Customer Rule: *A customer is considered a silver customer if the customer places 2-11 large orders during a half-calendar-year period that are each fully paid within 90 days.*

These three inference rules follow a pattern, as captured by the decision table (not complete) in Table 1. Creating a well-formed decision table for these rules is natural and mercifully eliminates much writing and reading (if represented and interpreted correctly).

Table 1. *Decision Table for Determining the Preference Level of a Customer*

Number of Orders Placed	Period of Time	Full Payment Timeframe	What is the Preference Level of a Customer?
48 or more	2 calendar years	45 days	platinum
12-47	1 calendar years	60 days	gold
2-11	half calendar year	90 days	silver

'Well-formed' means the decision table has clear and complete business semantics[30] – including but not limited to definitions and/or definitional rules for the terms it uses (i.e., customer, order, large order, etc.). It is essential that all decision tables be based on the same business vocabulary as all other elements of guidance so the complete set of guidance can be assessed holistically.

Inserting factual expressions into well-formed decision tables 'stamps' them as rules. The decision table above can be assumed to yield the following three logical implications:

48 or more orders AND during 2 calendar years AND fully paid within 45 days →

platinum customer

12-47 orders AND during 1 calendar year AND fully paid within 60 days →

gold customer

2-11 orders AND during a half calendar year AND fully paid within 90 days →

silver customer

30 For guidelines to create well-formed decision tables, refer to *Decision Tables – A Primer: How to Use TableSpeak™* (free download) http://www.brsolutions.com/publications/decision-tables-a-primer/

The Rule Messaging Triad Applied to Decision Tables

Chapter III-3 introduced the *Rule Messaging Triad*, comprising a rule, the rule's fact acquisition question(s), and the rule's guidance message(s). The focus of that chapter was mostly on behavioral rules and related definitional rules. The discussion below indicates how the Triad applies to decision tables.

Table 2 presents a decision table (not complete) including a set of three inference rules (one per row) each aimed at deciding the recommended delivery method for an order (the column on the far right) given different sets of facts (as indicated in the individual cells) using the same set of conditions (the top row).

Table 2. *Decision Table for Determining the Recommended Delivery Method for an Order*

rush order	*any fragile item*	*any specialty item*	*any high-priced item*	*any item involving hazardous materials*	*category of customer*	*destination of order*	***recommended delivery method for order***
no	*no*	*no*	*no*	*no*	*silver*	—	***picked up by customer***
yes	*yes*	*no*	*no*	*yes*	*gold*	*local*	***shipped by normal service***
yes	—	—	—	*yes*	*platinum*	*remote*	***shipped by premium service***

Rule Statements

The first leg of the Rule Messaging Triad is the rule itself.

Rules in decision tables are not expressed as statements. Rather, their meaning depends on the pattern established by the table. The individual rule statements are implicit.

Some platforms can produce such statements automatically, for example when a cursor is placed over the appropriate point in the table. Such tool-assisted verbalization can help communicate the assumed meaning of the rule for validation or other purposes. The rule statement for the second inference rule in the table, for example, might be expressed as:

> Rule Statement: *The recommended delivery method for an order is 'shipped by normal service' if all the following are true. The order:*
>
> - *is rush.*
> - *has a fragile item.*
> - *does not have a specialty item.*
> - *does not have a high-priced item.*
> - *has an item involving hazardous materials.*
> - *is placed by a gold customer.*
> - *is for a local destination.*

Fact Acquisition Questions

The second leg of the Rule Messaging Triad is fact acquisition questions(s).[31]

Since every rule in a decision table addresses the very same kinds of facts, a single set of fact acquisition questions (implicit or explicit) can normally serve for each and every rule in the table. For example, the following fact acquisition questions could serve for all the rules (currently three) in the decision table above:

- *Is the order rush?*
- *Does the order have a fragile item?*
- *Does the order have a specialty item?*
- *Does the order have a high-priced item?*
- *Does the order have an item involving hazardous materials?*
- *What is the category of the customer?*

[31] Interesting opportunities arise for using questions in multi-purpose, multi-directional interrogation of inference 'chains' (whether or not for inference rules in decision tables), but these opportunities are beyond the scope of the present discussion.

- *What is the destination of the order?*

Aside: Classical expert systems, by means of backward chaining, were often able to ask users for specific data needed to reach certain conclusions, even involving complex factual expressions. They could also often reveal why the data was being requested by exposing the chain of rules being evaluated.

Guidance Messages

The third leg of the Rule Messaging Triad is guidance messages(s).

Individual message(s) for any given rule in a decision table are possible, but usually not supported by current platforms. A general (evaluation-time) message for all the rules, however, might be useful. For example, a useful guidance message for the decision table above might be:

> Guidance Message: *Consider the recommended delivery method for an order to be the best decision under the circumstances unless pre-empted by more basic policies.*

Aside: Many practitioners don't realize there is no obligation to actually use or apply the result (outcome) from evaluating a decision table. The outcome in the decision table above is called '*recommended* delivery method for order' to emphasize this choice. Though the result is produced by definitional rules, those rules simply mean the result is necessarily what the rules indicate it to be. Whether or not the result is used in a process or activity is a separate question. For example, some knock-out rule(s) might prohibit using the result in certain circumstances. (Refer to Chapter IV-3.)

Appendix D

A Word About 'Decision'

Do all rules pertain to decisions? *Of course they do!*

- A behavioral rule provides criteria to decide whether or not behavior is appropriate.
- A definitional rule provides criteria to decide whether something counts as an instance of a concept.
- An inference rule in a decision table provides criteria to decide the correct outcome or choice under a specific set of circumstances.

But how helpful is that? 'Decision' can literally be applied to any choice you need to make anywhere, anytime – *whether or not explicit rules are at play.* For example, a decision could be:

- A highly consequential one-time strategic business decision (e.g., should our company do business in Africa?). Is it useful to codify decision logic for that?!
- A personal decision (e.g., not to stop at a red light). Do we need to crawl inside your head to replicate your logic?!
- A particular branch point in the code for an operating system. Does anyone but engineers need to concern themselves with that?!
- A statistically-based machine learning (ML) model is faced with a perception task (e.g., is this signature yours or not?). Does anyone in the business really care why it reaches its results?!

- Artificial intelligence (AI) inside a robot is faced with a mechanical task (e.g., whether it can lift a heavy, fragile object). Does anybody care except its creator?!

If you're reading this, I assume the challenge you face is organizing a group or community of people in business or government. With respect to such decisions as the above you're entitled to ask, *so what?!*

The challenge for groups and communities of people is rule-based governance. You need to know and understand rules, and be able to apply them in pinpoint fashion as far as possible in real time, allowing for insertion of human discretion, sentiment, and common sense.

Used without proper positioning, the term 'decision' has perverse generality. Be very careful about it.

Operational Business Decisions

To position our use of 'decision' properly, we instead carefully use the term 'operational business decision'. We are interested in decisions with respect to rules only where the decision:

- Pertains to groups and communities of people.
- Occurs repetitively in everyday activity.
- Can be based on explicit inference rules, especially in decision tables.

Such decisions can be quite complex and so require a structured approach to analysis.[32] Possible examples are:

- Should this insurance claim be accepted, rejected, or examined for fraud?
- Which resource should be assigned to this task?
- Which service should be used to ship this package?

---

[32] Our approach is called DecisionSpeak. Decision Analysis – *A Primer: How to Use DecisionSpeak™ and Question Charts (Q-Charts™)*, by Ronald G. Ross, 2013, available (free) on http://www.brsolutions.com/IPSpeakPrimers

Knock-out rules are directly relevant to operational business decisions. Refer to Chapter IV-3.

Delaying Operational Business Decisions to Optimize

Postponing an operational business decision (i.e., evaluation of the inference rules to 'decide it') until as late as possible in a process or procedure can optimize the results of the decision (*delaying-to-optimize*). OMG's BPMN (*Business Process Model and Notation*) for process logic, for example, allows decision logic to be invoked overtly at a given point in a process model.

Although the approach works for many (not all) operational business decisions, it doesn't work well at all for behavioral rules and all other definitional rules besides inference rules. *Real-time* evaluation of behavioral rules and related definitional rules is essential in maintaining ongoing guardrails (correctness) for activity and data.

Appendix E

Concept Models and Their Representation[33]

A concept model is a set of concepts structured according to the relations among them. That structure needs to be represented in a way that is formal and unambiguous. An SBVR-style structured business vocabulary does exactly that.[34]

In order to express rules or other statements about what can or should be, those statements cannot refer to data or to words, only to concepts. A concept model makes that possible by providing the underlying predicates.

With the clear exception of an SBVR-style structured business vocabulary, words alone are not a substitute for formal, logical representations of concepts. A typical business dictionary or business glossary cannot serve to represent a concept model in a formal way.

Intensions and Extensions

A concept model formally sets out what it means to be an instance of a given class of things. At a minimum, two questions must be answered:

1. What kind of thing is it?
2. What distinguishes it from other things?

The answers, known as the *intension* of the class, provide the necessary and sufficient conditions for something to be an instance. For example, suppose we say:

---

33 This Appendix co-authored with Mike Bennett.

34 Refer to *Business Knowledge Blueprints: Enabling Your Data to Speak the Language of the Business* (2nd ed), by Ronald G. Ross, 2020.

1. A set of things exists that is a mammal (itself a kind of vertebrate, and so on).
2. It is necessarily the case that to be a member of this set, a thing has expressive ears, a tail that wags, and a wet nose.

We've thereby given a (somewhat informal) description of the intension of all the things that are a dog. Note that we did not need to rely on the word 'dog' to categorize that kind of thing in the world.

In set theoretic terms, the set of things that matches the criteria in the intension form the *extension* of that set. I actually have one of those dog-ish things in my backyard named 'Rita'. Rita is very real. Sometimes, however, the concept model informs you about things that cannot exist (i.e., are impossible). In some respects, distinguishing between things that can exist and that cannot exist is equally important.

Intensional definitions necessarily reference other kinds of thing included in the same model. In all, a concept model provides an internally consistent understanding of the things relevant to the business.

Ontologies

This kind of model is often referred to as an ontology. Caution must be exercised about that word for at least two reasons:

- Some things called an ontology do not represent the real things in the world, but rather define a set of data elements that represent those things.
- By definition, any model that allows for framing a formal set of intensional definitions of things is an ontology. The formalism must, however, be able to express those things unambiguously.

Many ontologies use a textual representation of logic such as Description Logic (DL) or First Order Logic (FOL). These statements may be expressed using logical expressions that contain special symbols such ∀ as or ∃.

Ontologies are also used to represent meanings in linked data or knowledge graphs – for example using Web Ontology Language (OWL) from the W3C. Although such models are ontologies, they are not concept models since they represent data.

Since OWL supports the same formalisms as Description Logic, OWL could in principle be used to express a concept model. The construction of such a model would be very different, however, than an OWL ontology used to reason over data. Any use of OWL for a concept model should therefore make it very clear that the things it represents are real things, not data.

The field of formal ontology encompasses many variations and exceptions to what has been described above. For example, some ontology frameworks reject the very notion of 'concept' and represent things only in some real or possible world (called 'ontological realism'). Others avoid intensions and provide only extensional definitions of things.

Higher-Order Expressions

The world is not limited just to what can be defined with a first-order or declarative kind of logical statement. A concept model provides the building blocks for such higher-order logical expressions.

Especially important for groups and communities of people are expressions based on deontic modal logic (including behavioral rules, permissions, authorizations, and rights). See Appendix F. Such expressions are not, however, part of a concept model per se.

Data Models

Why do we use the term 'concept model' rather than 'conceptual model'? The term 'conceptual model' is not incorrect, but also may not be useful.

In software development and data modeling, it is common practice for developers to take a representation of some logical data model, cross out all the 'difficult' bits, and present it to the business as a 'conceptual model'. The false implication is that the world of the business is somehow simpler than the world of information technology.

In reality, every business and knowledge specialty is highly complex. A concept model can easily be more complex than any corresponding data model. Indeed, a good data model or design usually simplifies the complexities of the real world. A concept model is not an abstraction of a logical data model; it is a rigorous model of how things in reality are understood.

Appendix F

Modalities: Forms of Guidance

The complete set of forms of guidance based on modal logic is as follows.[35] Assume the modal operator is applied to a proposition that corresponds to a state of affairs. The meaning of the proposition is independent of any form of expression.

Table 1. *Forms of Guidance Based on Modality*

Kind of Modal Logic	*Modality Applied to Proposition*	*Effect on Corresponding State of Affairs*	*Is the Guidance a Rule?*	*Example*
Deontic	obligation	obligated	yes	*You are obligated to bring a dish to the picnic.*
	prohibition	prohibited		*You are prohibited from bringing alcohol to the picnic.*
	non-obligation	permitted or prohibited	no	*You are not obligated to swim at the picnic. (It might be prohibited though.)*
	permission (non-prohibition)	permitted or obligated		*You are permitted to wear a company shirt to the picnic. (It might be obligated though.)*
	optionality	not obligated and not prohibited		*You are permitted to bring a friend to the picnic, but it's not obligated.*
Alethic	necessity	necessary	yes	*A shirt for this restaurant always has sleeves.*
	impossibility	impossible		*A shirt for this restaurant is never without a tail long enough to be tucked inside the waistband of trousers or a skirt.*
	non-necessity	possible or impossible	no	*A shirt for this restaurant can have holes in it. (Such a garment might not be a shirt for this restaurant though.)*
	possibility	possible or necessary		*A shirt for this restaurant can have a collar. (A collar might be necessary though.)*
	contingency	not necessary and not impossible		*A shirt for this restaurant can either have pockets or no pockets.*

35 based on SBVR Table 24.2

Conflicts Among Modal Operators

Modal conflicts in guidance cannot be allowed to stand. For example, alethic modalities 'win' over deontic modalities:

- What is necessary cannot be prohibited.
- What is impossible cannot be obligated.

On the other hand, certain modalities are not inherently in conflict. A permission pertaining to some state of affairs does not conflict with an obligation for that same state of affairs. Obviously, if something is obligated it has to be permitted.

> *Aside:* But in an optimistic world, why retain expressions of both in the same body of guidance? The explicit permission is not needed (and possibly confusing). The same is not true, however, for authorizations (permissions in a pessimistic world). In that case, something cannot be obligated unless it is specifically authorized. So, if something authorized is obligated, both expressions are needed.

Conflicts among model operators are given by Tables 2 and 3.

Table 2. *Conflicts Among Deontic Modalities*

✓ - not in conflict
X - conflict

Deontic Modalities	obligation	non-obligation	optionality	permission (non-prohibition)	prohibition
obligation		X	X	✓	X
non-obligation	X		✓	✓	✓
optionality	X	✓		✓	X
permission (non-prohibition)	✓	✓	✓		X
prohibition	X	✓	X	X	

Table 3. *Conflicts Among Alethic Modalities*

✓ - not in conflict

X - conflict

Alethic Modalities	necessity	non-necessity	contingency	non-impossibility	impossibility
necessity		X	X	✓	X
non-necessity	X		✓	✓	✓
contingency	X	✓		✓	X
non-impossibility	✓	✓	✓		X
impossibility	X	✓	X	X	

Appendix G

Positive Reinforcement and Rewards

Behavioral rules in particular aim at ensuring real-time correctness of business behavior (and therefore quality of data). So, they naturally focus on detecting violations in real time, along with negative sanctions or feedback. The larger objective, however, is to shape behavior in desired ways. For that reason, *positive* sanctions or feedback could sometimes be useful for *correctly* complying with some behavioral rule(s).

Such positive reinforcement could be used to encourage or sustain engagement. (Who doesn't like the occasional treat for acting properly, especially while learning?!) Positive reinforcement might be as simple as an acknowledgement message or icon (👍) or more substantial, in the form of some reward.

Just as for detecting violations, the flash points for rules are key in supporting positive reinforcement. Specifically, when a rule is evaluated, if none of its flash points 'flash' (i.e., indicate a fault), then the rule has been followed properly.

For positive reinforcement and rewards, the usual terminology associated with rule evaluation (see Chapter I-4) requires adjustment, for example:

- Instead of 'guidance message', a 'compliance confirmation' could be sent.
- Instead of a 'violation response', a 'compliance reward' could be invoked.

Monitoring Compliance by Actor

The performance of any actor(s) in complying with some rule(s) can be monitored over time. Such performance indicators not only can measure failures (instances of violations), but successes (instances of compliance) as well. Such indicators could be used to gauge the skill level or the disruptiveness of any particular actor(s).

Appendix H

Sample Enforcement Levels for Behavioral Rules

This table suggests a set of enforcement levels aimed at automated real-time activity (i.e., where attempted violations can be detected in real time).

Enforcement Level	***Description***	***Implications***
strictly enforced	If an actor violates the rule, the actor cannot escape the consequences and possible penalties.	When a violation is detected, results from the event producing the violation are automatically prevented. (Special provisions may be required for time-based rules since the procession of time cannot be prevented. Such provisions might, for example, involve freezing some actor's access privileges, halting some workflow, etc.)
deferred enforcement	The rule is strictly enforced, but such enforcement may be delayed – e.g., until another actor with required skills and proper authority can become involved.	When a violation is detected, results from the event producing the violation are handed off to another worker for resolution (possibly by insertion into a work queue).
override by privileged actor	The rule is enforced, but an actor with special privilege established before the fact may override it.	When a violation is detected, if the actor involved is specially privileged, that actor is given an opportunity to override the rule.
override with real-time waiver	The rule is enforced, but an actor may request a real-time waiver from another actor having before-the-fact authority to give such waivers.	When a violation is detected, the actor involved is given an opportunity to interactively request a waiver from pre-defined authority.
post-justified override	The rule may be overridden by an actor; however, if the override is subsequently deemed inappropriate, the actor may be subject to penalty.	When an override of a rule occurs, a review item (with all relevant details) should be inserted into the work queue of an appropriate actor for review and possible action.
override with explanation	The rule may be overridden simply by providing a reasonable explanation.	When a violation is detected, the actor involved is given an opportunity to override the rule by providing a mandatory explanation.
guideline	Suggested, but not enforced.	When a violation is detected, the actor involved is simply informed/reminded of the rule by some guidance message(s).

Notes

1. The set of enforcement levels is not appropriate for all automated activity (e.g., where data is transferred between different businesses or government bodies).
2. For this set of enforcement levels, any attempted violation is assumed to result in an actual violation (even if corrected in real time). This default might not be preferred for some or all enforcement levels, or for other sets of enforcement levels.
3. All violations should be logged for potential subsequent review. Overrides and waivers by actor and rule should also be logged.
4. Contrast overrides with authorizations, under which no violation occurs for authorized actors.
5. In the case of deferred enforcement or overrides, additional rules giving timing criteria may be desirable to ensure some action is taken within an appropriate timeframe.

Appendix I

Warranties

The air conditioning in my office is always breaking down. Believe me, where I live you need it to work (and think and just live). Fortunately, I have a warranty. When the A/C breaks down, I have recourse. What is it that I actually have?

A *warranty* is a promise by the maker of a statement that the statement is true. Since a warranty is a promise, it can be breached (unlike a representation).[36] Something that can be breached (violated) represents a behavioral rule. ('Something' in this discussion always specifically means 'some state of affairs'.)

Suppose the warranty promises my A/C equipment will operate correctly for five years. Putting that promise into rule-ish form produces:

> Five-Year Rule: *My A/C equipment must operate correctly for five years.*

The rule creates an obligation for manufacturer of the A/C equipment. Once a warranty is understood as an obligation, it can be written:

> Warranty: *My A/C equipment will operate correctly for five years.*

Now suppose my A/C equipment breaks down in three years. What's my remedy? Let's suppose the manufacturer has agreed as part of the warranty that if the equipment fails irreparably within five years, it will replace the equipment free of charge.

This promise is also a rule, which can be expressed in several ways, including either of the following.

---

[36] Drafting Contracts: *How and Why Lawyers Do What They Do*, Tina L. Stark, Wolters Kluwer, Aspen Publishers, 2007, p. 13, 16. (*See CBS, Inc. v. Ziff-Davis Publg.* Co., 554 N.Y.S.2d 449, 452-453 (1990).)

Remedy Rule: *The manufacturer must replace the equipment free of charge.*

Warranty: *The manufacturer will replace the equipment free of charge.*

Even though agreed, this Remedy Rule is not enforced until and unless the equipment fails irreparably within five years – in other words, the original promise is breached. A breach means the Five-Year Rule has been violated. So, the Remedy Rule should be treated as a violation response for the Five-Year Rule. (See Chapter I-4.)

Aside: Legally, a breach does occur and needs to be recognized as such. Just expressing the warranty logic in one or more IF-THEN statements, though perhaps it could be made to work, fails to reflect the reality of a violation.

Let's assume that 'remedy' is always understood as a violation response. The overall treatment of the entire warranty boils down to simply:

Warranty: My A/C equipment will operate correctly for five years.

Remedy: The manufacturer will replace the equipment free of charge if irreparable.

A rule treated as a violation response for another rule depends directly on the meaning of the other rule. It can't be decoupled. Therefore, the expression of any rule that acts as a violation response is considered face-value trustworthy. To emphasize the point, the Remedy could also be expressed:

Remedy: *If the Warranty is violated, the manufacturer will replace the equipment free of charge if irreparable.*

Appendix J

Usage Constraints for Applicability Conditions

An applicability condition is a criterion or condition under which a behavioral rule has a different enforcement level, violation response(s), and/or guidance message(s) than in some other case(s). Applicability conditions permit highly-nuanced responses to violations – that is, situational sensitivity and situational awareness.

Special constraints apply to use of applicability conditions as follow:

- An applicability condition must extend the base rule by adding some condition(s). The applicability condition cannot broaden the coverage of the base rule (create a superset of cases); it must always narrow the base rule's coverage (create a subset of cases).
- Once an applicability condition is specified, enforcement level can no longer be specified directly for the base rule. Instead, at least two applicability conditions must be specified (all mutually exclusive) so no conflicts in enforcement level arise.
- Distinct sets of applicability conditions can be specified for guidance messages or violation actions.

Definitional rules (including inference rules) can assist in expressing applicability conditions. For example, an applicability condition might include a term that is rule-based in the sense of being derived or calculated.

More complex applicability conditions for some behavioral rule(s) might be supported by sets of inference rules (e.g., decision tables). Such sets of rules would support dynamic settings based on context, time, or other criteria.

Appendix K

Why Not Use IF-THEN Syntax

As discussed in Chapter II-3, ruleness never happens by accident. The ruleness of a factual expression has to be overtly 'stamped' onto it. Why not use the IF-THEN syntax for that purpose in rules for groups and communities of people? The following discussion identifies a half-dozen compelling reasons for why not.

Although the discussion focuses on IF-THEN syntax, it should be noted that WHEN-THEN syntax has all the same problems for rules *and more*. Specifically, the WHEN part of an expression can easily refer to an event, not some fact(s). (Otherwise, why not say "IF" instead of "WHEN"?) Some rules are indeed intended for enforcement only upon a given event, but such rules represent a small minority. More likely, the event referenced after the WHEN is simply one of the two or more flash points for the rule, probably the most obvious. Refer to Appendix N.

Also note that sets of patterned inference rules (often expressed in IF-THEN syntax individually) should be represented in decision tables, removing concerns about sentence syntax altogether. Refer to Appendix C.

Reason 1. The first reason has to do with effective human communication, nothing whatsoever with automation. No matter how obsessed the world has become with automation, putting the IF part of a rule first in a rule statement is simply not good writing style for formal communication.

A rule statement is often loaded with qualifications. Using IF-THEN syntax, those qualifications all come at the start of the sentence, taxing the reader's memory and concentration. Which of the following two versions of the same rule would you prefer to read?

Front-Loaded Rule Version Using IF-THEN:

If a company is located in a country suspected of terrorist activity and a machine is owned by an employee included in a team assigned to a high-security project, then the machine is not to be serviced by the company.

Back-Loaded Rule Version Avoiding THEN:

A machine is not to be serviced by a company if the company is located in a country suspected of terrorist activity and the machine is owned by an employee included in a team assigned to a high-security project.

The first version shows no mercy on the reader's short-term memory. The THEN part is what the reader needs first, as in the second version. That part anchors all the qualifications.

This structure is clearly the best approach for behavioral rules and related definitional rules. As Steven Pinker says, "Putting the heavy material last is [one] of the most important guidelines for good style in writing."[37]

Reason 2. Contrary to popular belief – a belief encouraged by programming languages and many software platforms – an IF-THEN statement does not automatically make a rule.

In logic, an IF-THEN statement expresses an implication (often written A → B, or A implies B). But implications come in two forms – material implication and logical implication.

- A *material* implication is true when all available evidence (data) supports it. But maybe you just haven't come across a black swan yet – in other words, your knowledge or data is incomplete. "If swan, then white." Don't trust it as a rule!

37 *The Stuff of Thought*, by Steven Pinker, Viking, 2007, p. 74.

- A *logical* implication requires commitment or expression of intent. You must stipulate that you meant there will be no black swans. In other words, you must 'stamp' the expression "If swan, then white." with ruleness. Refer to Chapter II-3.

IF-THEN alone does *not* accomplish such 'stamping' of ruleness – unless your programming language or software platform makes a built-in assumption. Such assumptions are inappropriate, of course, for formal business communication.

Reason 3. IF-THEN is often unnatural for behavioral rules. Try your hand at casting the following statement into IF-THEN form: *A minor must be accompanied by an adult.* The result is probably something like: *If a person is a minor, then that person must be accompanied by an adult.* Is that how we talk and write? No, not at all.

Reason 4. IF-THEN is awkward for basic definitional rules. Suppose you stipulate as a rule: *A mammal has hair.* As an IF-THEN statement, it becomes: *If mammal, then hair.* If *what* is a mammal?! Hair having to do with *what?!* The result seems like some kind of shorthand. *Why?!* The original version already said exactly what you meant.

Reason 5. Rules need to be expressed factually so they can focus on what needs to be true, not what actions should be taken. (Refer to Chapters II-2 and II-3 for examples and discussion.) It is all too tempting to specify an action or command after the THEN part of an IF-THEN statement thereby producing a conditional instruction.

Reason 6. From a business perspective, software engineers often address the wrong things after the THEN part of behavioral rules expressed using IF-THEN. These things include reactions to, or messages about, violations of the rule. As a result, rule statements become badly distorted. Consider the following simple example:

Rule: *An employee must have a name.*

To support this rule, a software engineer might write:

Software Engineer Version: *If an employee does not have a name, then set error flag.*

This programming statement indicates the action 'set error flag' after the THEN part. That particular action is of no interest to a business person; it's simply the programming reaction to the detection of a violation.

Also, the software engineer is looking for violations of the rule. So, for the programming logic to work properly, the 'must have' in the original rule has become 'does *not* have'. The business logic is reversed from its natural form.

Had the logic involved a threshold comparison, the reversal would be even more distorting. For example, a 'greater than' would become a 'less than or equal to'. The result is a major disconnect in communication with business people. Business people often go silent, software engineers fail to understand why, and everyone ends up frustrated.

Appendix L

The Relationship of Facts and Data

Today we are absolutely consumed by talk of data and being data-driven. For AI, everything is data – images, video feeds, acoustics, free-form text, you name it. Elaborate data architectures are all the rage. 'Data' is so much in our heads and in our discourse, sometimes it seems there is hardly any room left to think about 'facts'. Does there even need to be?

Yes! For the sake of rules. And for the sake of knowledge. And for the sake of no less than the quality of the very data itself.

Actually, facts and structured data (the kind you typically find in databases) are intimately related. The gap between them is probably not at all what you think it might be. Let's explore the matter.

Suppose I ask you for an example of a city. You respond with "Utrecht." I trust you, so I accept Utrecht as a city. Because my memory is bad, I put it in a database for safekeeping. What just happened?

We had an exchange of messages, of course. This exchange might have been in person or digital, no matter. Now I have the piece of data 'Utrecht' in my database. I have other cities represented there too, including 'New York', 'Tokyo', 'Singapore', etc.

When I put 'Utrecht' in my database, I obviously didn't put in the *real* city (way too big to fit). I put in just the name of the city, the character string that acts as a signifier for the real city.

How should I interpret that piece of data? I originally asked for an example of a city. You sent me back "Utrecht." So actually, your message can be properly interpreted as "Utrecht is an example of a city." In other words, you sent me a *fact*, even though your message wasn't a complete sentence. 'Utrecht' in my database is actually a representation of that original fact, in shorthand form, inserted into the database to assist memory.

You should think of every piece of data in every cell of every database table as representing some fact (many more complicated than this one). Structured data is not just data; it represents assertions of facts – a basic form of knowledge.[38]

We hope the assertions in the database are true. We hope they are reliable and we can trust them. Unfortunately, there are no guarantees apart from rules.

[38] For more about how ambiguity arises in data, refer to Appendix 1 of *Business Knowledge Messaging: How to Avoid Business Miscommunication*, by Ronald G. Ross, 2022

Appendix M

Structural Forms of Expression for Rules

To be communicated to a group or community of people, the meaning of a rule must be expressed clearly, usually in some form of controlled natural language. Although the same rule can often be expressed in many ways in the same natural language, all such rule expressions fall into a very limited set of structural forms, as outlined below.

Behavioral Rule Statements

A behavioral rule can be expressed in exactly three forms, with the indicated consequences for a corresponding state of affairs:[39]

Form of Behavioral Rule Statement	***Effect on Corresponding State of Affairs***	***Sample Sentence Form***	***Sample Rule Expression***
obligation statement	obligated	... must ...	*Every person must wear a hard hat on their head while in a construction site.*
prohibition statement	prohibited	... must not ...	*A retired employee must not have an employment counselor.*
restricted permission statement	permitted only under certain conditions	... is permitted ... only ...	*An employee is permitted an employment counselor only if the employee is not retired.*

The last two examples given in the table have exactly the same meaning. The equivalence of a rule expressed as a prohibition statement to the same meaning expressed as a restricted permission statement is dictated by logic.

39 from SBVR, Clause 18.2.1

Definitional Rule Statements

A definitional rule can be expressed in exactly three forms, with the indicated consequences for a corresponding state of affairs:[40]

Form of Definitional Rule Statement	***Effect on Corresponding State of Affairs***	***Sample Sentence Form***	***Sample Rule Expression***
necessity statement	necessary	... always ...	*A reservation always has a reservation holder.*
impossibility statement	impossible	... cannot ...	*The pick-up branch of a one-way rental cannot be the return branch of that rental.*
restricted possibility statement	possible only under certain conditions	... can ... only ...	*The pick-up branch of a rental can be the return branch of that rental only if the rental is not one-way.*

The last two examples given in the table have exactly the same meaning. The equivalence of a rule expressed as an impossibility statement to the same meaning expressed as a restricted possibility statement is dictated by logic.

40

Appendix N

Use of 'WHEN'

Single-Event Rules

As mentioned in Chapter III-2, a small minority of rules are legitimately evaluated only upon a single flash point. Use of 'when' in these cases is altogether appropriate. Some examples.

> Single-Event Rule: *A notification message must be sent to the customer <u>when</u> an order arrives at the destination.*

This example involves only a single flash point: *when the order arrives at the destination*. In this case, it would make no sense for the rule to also cover the event *when an order <u>leaves</u> the destination.*

> *Reminder:* Rules should never refer to actions. The verb 'sent' in the above rule is used in the indicative (factual) mood, not imperative mood.

> Single-Event Rule: *An advisor for a student must be a teacher teaching some course that student currently takes <u>when</u> the advisor is selected for the student.*

Assuming the rule correctly captures the business intent, the school apparently wants a teacher-student connection only at the time the advisor is selected. It does not deem continuation of that connection important thereafter. For example, in future terms or semesters the advisor might not teach any course the student takes.

> Single-Event Rule: *No shirt, no service <u>when</u> a customer enters the restaurant.*

Based on what might happen *after* a customer enters the restaurant, this restaurant might sport some highly unusual on-premises behavior(!).

'When' vs. 'If'

In some current rule platforms and languages, 'when' and 'if' are used more or less interchangeably to introduce a qualification (condition) in a rule statement. We recommend against that practice for the obvious reason that 'when' is more naturally used to specifically reference events. Since rules occasionally are specific to a given event (as above), we reserve 'when' for that special case.

'When' and Flash Points

Let's return to the simple example examined at the beginning of Chapter III-2.

Rule: *A customer must have an address.*

As before, this rule has two flash points:

- When a new customer arises (is created).
- When the address of an existing customer is eliminated (is deleted).

Since these two expressions represent flash points, not the rule per se, it would be odd and highly counterproductive to include them in expressing the rule itself. In fact, excluding flash points where not specifically relevant to the business intent of a rule is critical to being declarative rather than procedural about rules. (Refer to Chapter II-2.)

For this reason, you should always inspect any rule very carefully that includes a 'when' clause. Such a statement is likely not expressing the rule's true intent. For example:

Rule: *A customer must have an address* when *the customer is created.*

As above, what about two seconds later? Can the address be deleted? This revised version doesn't say it can't be. Although the 'when' qualification in the statement is true, it renders the rule's coverage incomplete. Now another statement is needed to cover the second flash point:

Rule: *A customer must have an address* when *the customer is updated.*

Using 'when' in this fashion has at least two undesirable consequences.

1. Where originally there was a single rule, now there are two. In other words, the number of rules has doubled. Managing more rules than absolutely necessary is highly unproductive. And remember, many rules actually have more than two flash points. Creating rule surrogates for each of a rule's flash points is one reason why sets of rules often multiply in size unnecessarily. Don't confuse rules and flash points. They are not the same!
2. The expression of these flash-specific rules has become unfriendly and unnatural.
    - '*Create* a customer'?! Try to imagine a flesh-and-blood customer being created right there on the spot. *Really?!*
    - '*Update* a customer'?! Imagine a real-life customer standing in front of you being updated. *Cosmetic surgery anyone?!*

That's simply not the kind of language that business people use to talk about real-world things. Instead, the specifications are now about events occurring for a *representation* of the real-life customer *in a data store.* We've switched to DataSpeak or SystemSpeak.

That switch might be acceptable for specifying the flash points for a rule; it is highly undesirable for specifying the rule itself. For this reason, the 'CRUD' words 'create', 'retrieve', 'update', and 'delete' are never recommended for expressing rules in business communication.

Appendix O

Flash Points and Definitional Rules

A flash point is a real-time event in business activity that attempts to change a state of affairs relevant to one or more rules. All definitional rules, including inference rules, generally have two or more flash points just like behavioral rules.

Consider the logical implication A → B (an inference rule). Its two flash points are:

- When A becomes true. (B becomes true.)
- When B becomes false. (A becomes false.)

In theory, all definitional rules could be automatically evaluated in real time at each of its flash points. (Whether the rule proves true or false might remain unknown if some relevant fact(s) is/are missing). As discussed later, however, real-time evaluation is not always desirable.

Definitional Rules Associated with Behavioral Rules

Real-time assessment of definitional rules can cause violations of behavioral rules. Here are several examples.

- Consider the No-Shirt, No-Service Rule. Suppose a customer already seated in a restaurant suddenly rips the sleeves off their shirt. The definitional rule has nothing to say about whether a customer may vandalize their shirt – that would be a behavioral rule. Now, however, the garment no longer counts as a shirt, so the customer is immediately in violation of the No-Shirt, No-Service Rule. Evaluation of the definitional rule has acted as an extended flash point for evaluation of the behavioral rule.

- Consider the rule: *A customer is to be assigned an agent if the customer has placed an order.* Suppose a definitional rule indicates that an agent is always an employee of the company. One day the agent's relationship changes from employee to contract basis. The definitional rule has nothing to say about whether an agent may switch relationships with the company – that would be a behavioral rule. Now, however, the person no longer counts as an agent, so a violation of the above behavioral rule immediately occurs. Again, evaluation of the definitional rule has acted as an extended flash point for evaluation of a behavioral rule.

In short, real-time evaluation of definitional rules is especially important where they directly support behavioral rules.

Delayed Evaluations of Definitional Rules Associated with Behavioral Rules

Real-time evaluation of definitional rules associated with behavioral rules, however, is not always possible. Here are several examples.

- Consider the No-Shirt, No-Service Rule. Suppose a customer comes to the restaurant wearing highly unusual garb on the upper part of their body. Probably confounded, the host seats the customer. Later, the manager eyes the shirt and makes a determination that the garb does not qualify as a shirt. Now, the customer is 'suddenly' in violation of the behavioral rule and should be denied service. In this case, a delayed assessment of the definitional rules for 'shirt' causes the behavioral rule to come into play. In effect, evaluation of the definitional rules results in a late 'flash'.

- Consider a suspicious death. After examining the remains, the coroner rules 'homicide'. The homicide has already occurred, of course, but it is ruled as such only after the fact. Again, delayed assessment of the definitional rules for 'homicide' as a cause of death brings the behavioral rule about murder into play. In effect, evaluation of the definitional rules results in a late 'flash'.

Real-Time Evaluation of Definitional Rules for Non-Rule Reasons

Real-time evaluation of definitional rules at any or all of its flash points sometimes might be desirable for business or system reasons. For example, a message might be displayed to a customer when the customer becomes eligible for a certain discount. Assuming there's no behavioral rule about notifying the customer, doing so is just deemed a desirable business prompt or system feature.

Delayed Evaluation of Definitional Rules for Practical Reasons

In practice, evaluation for many definitional rules tends to occur on an as-used basis. For example, a definitional rule that computes a numerical result might be evaluated only when the result is needed by an actor, decision, or process rather than continuously (which could degrade system performance).

Evaluation of inference rules (definitional rules often found in decision tables) typically occurs only when an actor or process requests a decision. Deferring evaluation in this manner often optimizes operational business decisions and thereby improves business performance (*delaying-to-optimize*). For more, refer to Appendix D.

Appendix P

Eliminating Programmer Workload for Rules

These days we can automate operational business decisions reasonably well using decision models and decision tables. Not perfectly, but tolerably well. Coding that kind of business logic can be off-loaded from programmers to existing rule platforms.

But programmers are still responsible for another kind of rule-related coding – one that consumes not only huge amounts of resources, but that has profound impact for both quality of service and quality of data. They must code everything having to do with behavioral rules. That's far more than you might imagine!

Let's explore the matter by looking at a sample behavioral rule. The partial concept model diagram shown in Figure 1 illustrates the vocabulary the rule uses.

> Agent Rule: *A customer must be assigned to an agent if the customer has placed an order.*

Figure 1. *Partial Concept Model Diagram for the Agent Rule*

In the diagram:

- noun concepts are indicated using boxes labeled by terms.
- verb concepts are indicated using worded lines and arrows.

The rule has been expressed in a purely declarative manner. (See Chapter II-2.) So, the rule does not indicate any process, procedure, or other means to enforce or apply it.

Now ask yourself: Why would I need any process model whatsoever to enforce it?! A human can understand and enforce the rule properly without any reference to a process model. So why couldn't a machine?!

In today's world, a huge amount of programmer workload comes from building process models and writing code to enforce behavioral rules. It's a *massive* workload. There are literally 1,000s of behavioral rules in a business or government of any size or complexity – probably 10,000s or more.

The impact for programmer workload falls into two categories – event detection and event management – as discussed below.

Event Detection

The first category of impact for programmer workload is event detection. Note that the Agent Rule makes no reference whatsoever to any event when the rule could be potentially violated or needs to be evaluated. The rule expression for example does *not* say, "When a customer places an order, then [do something]."

That observation is extremely important for the following reason. 'When a customer places an order' is not the only event when the rule could potentially be violated and therefore needs to be evaluated. There is another event when the rule could potentially be violated: 'When an agent leaves our company...'. When an agent leaves, their assigned customers can be left high and dry, violating the rule. So, the rule needs to be evaluated at that kind of event as well.

In other words, the Agent Rule could potentially be violated during two quite distinct kinds of operational event:

- The first, 'When a customer places an order ...', is rather obvious.
- The second, 'When an agent leaves our company ...', might be much less so.

Both events are nonetheless important because either could potentially produce a violation. As discussed in Chapter III-2, these clear-cut events are the rule's *flash points*.

> *Remember:* Definitional criteria might also apply. If some fact(s) about an agent change such that the person no longer counts as an agent (according to the definition and/or definitional rules for 'agent'), such event could also produce a violation of the behavioral rule. Think of these events as extended flash points for the Agent Rule.

Like the Agent Rule, the large majority of rules have at least two flash points; many have more (but usually not more than four or five). Also as for the Agent Rule, one or more of the flash points are often subtle.

> *Aside:* If you like to think in terms of decisions, ask yourself what operational business decision that second flash point for the Agent Rule corresponds to?! Perhaps you could invent one for the purpose, but it wouldn't be very natural from a business point of view.

Ask yourself this additional question: What in current IT approaches and tools ensures you will get consistent results for the rule across all the processes, procedures, and use cases where all its flash points might occur? And don't forget about ad hoc activity; that is, lightly scripted or even unscripted activity.

Unfortunately, the answer today is almost *nothing*. If the job gets done at all, it's a job for programmers. In other words, it's programmer workload.

And since it's a programmer responsibility, it's error-prone. It produces brittle systems that are hard to maintain, especially when rules change. It's also a big reason why data quality is so poor in many organizations.

Event Management

The second category of impact for programmer workload is event management. Let's use soccer to illustrate and analyze the enforcement of behavioral rules. Well-known behavioral rules in soccer include *offsides* and no tackling *from behind*. These rules are evaluated by a referee watching the ongoing activity and judging in real time when there is a violation.

There is no process model needed for playing a game of soccer. What a strange notion that would be!

Instead, for enforcement of behavioral rules, soccer features a referee, which I call the *watcher*, who is external to the activity and able to interrupt it at any time. Detection of, and responses to, violations of behavioral rules occur in real time.

The notion of *real-time* intervention for enforcement of behavioral rules is critical. As in soccer, you simply can't wait to a later point in the activity to enforce many (or most) behavioral rules because by then it's too late. The harm done by a violation can compound itself many times over.

A suitable rule platform for business and government would remove 'watching' as yet another programmer responsibility. What a huge boost for productivity, consistent experience, and data quality that would be!

Fun Thought: In the case of a complex potential violation in soccer, the referee could interrupt the game and call the VAR (Video Assistant Referee) to confirm/disconfirm the violation. Could such things happen in business activity!? *Why not!*

Appendix Q

Definitions, Rules, and Logical Implications

Logical implication is not a notion that policy writers and business analysts need to understand or address directly. Their work needs to be kept as simple as possible (because it's already *not* simple!). They need to remain focused on semantic questions arising from the textual business statements at hand.

Logical implication is, however, a crucial notion in logic, fundamental for verifying the logical consistency of a knowledgebase and for implementing reasoners. This appendix explains how logical implications relate to:[41]

- Definitions
- Definitional rules
- Conditional definitional rules
- Behavioral rules

In reading this discussion, remember that a term is a designation for a concept, not the concept itself. Similarly, a definition is a representation of a concept, not the concept itself either. A concept is always in the mind. Logical implications can imply nothing about what is in your mind, only things having to do with the terms and definitions themselves.

---

[41] For more about logical implications and inferences refer to: Donald E. Baisley, Keri Anderson Healy, and Ronald G. Ross, "SBVR Support for Inference: Logical Effects of Claims of Necessity and Obligation on Implications", *Business Rules Journal* Vol. 20, No. 4, (Apr. 2019) URL: http://www.brcommunity.com/a2019/b988.html

Definitions

Assume only a definition is given for a term, no definitional rule(s). In that case, the term implies the definition and the definition implies the term. Example of a term and its (short) definition:

bachelor: *an unmarried adult male*

This meaning can be expressed as a bidirectional logical implication:

bachelor ←→ unmarried adult male

A bi-directional implication is implicit in any term and definition pair (where no definitional rules apply). Suppose we have a very simple definition of 'shirt':

shirt: *a garment for the upper part of the body*

This meaning can again be expressed as a bidirectional logical implication:

shirt ←→ garment for the upper part of the body

As previously discussed, this definition is inadequate for the No-Shirt, No-Service Rule (and probably other uses as well), so additional definitional criteria are likely needed.

Definitional Rules

A definitional rule is always considered part of the meaning of some concept. The definitional rule has been externalized from the definition of the concept for the convenience of writers and readers. Why? The definitional rule might provide some fine-grained precision that an approachable definition lacks. Or there may be so many refinements in the meaning of a concept that including them all in its definition is impractical.

For example, suppose greater precision is desired for the definition of 'shirt' above. So, the following definitional rule is specified:

What's-a-Shirt Rule: *A shirt has sleeves and a tail long enough to be tucked inside the waistband of trousers or a skirt.*

This meaning can be expressed as a uni-directional logical implication:

shirt → sleeves AND tail long enough to be tucked inside the waistband of trousers or a skirt

This logical implication is not bi-directional because it lacks what the definition says, "garment for the upper part of the body."

Also, now that we've added the definitional rule, the original definition itself is no longer bi-directional:

shirt → garment for the upper part of the body

Only when you add the definitional rule and the definition together does the logical implication become bi-directional:

shirt ←→ garment for the upper part of the body AND sleeves AND tail long enough to be tucked inside the waistband of trousers or a skirt

Conditional Definitional Rules

Definitional rules are often conditional. The condition naturally establishes a logical implication. Consider the following definition and definitional rule for 'gold customer'.

gold customer: *a customer that places substantial orders over a sustained period of time*

Gold Customer Rule: *A customer is considered a gold customer if the customer places more than 12 large orders during a calendar year that are each fully paid within 60 days.*

Since the rule is conditional, it naturally establishes a logical implication:

customer places more than 12 large orders during a calendar year that are each fully paid within 60 days → gold customer

Since a separate definition has been given, this logical implication alone could not possibly be bi-directional. (It makes no difference whether or not the conditional logical implication happens to appear in a decision table.)

For rule-based terms such as 'gold customer', the definitional rule alone may sometimes be deemed sufficient for the concept (no definition needed). For example, suppose it's decided that the definition of 'gold customer' above doesn't really add much. If the definition is discarded, then the logical implication itself becomes bi-directional (assuming the logic is complete):

gold customer ←→ customer places more than 12 large orders during a calendar year that are each fully paid within 60 days

Behavioral Rules

The key characteristic of behavioral rules is that they can be violated. Therefore, *they never produce inferences* even if conditional. Example:[42]

Behavioral Rule: *It is obligatory that a branch office is closed between the hours of 1AM and 5AM.*

This rule would seem to suggest the following inference:

time is between 1AM and 5AM → branch office is closed

No. Suppose that the current time is 3AM. Any given branch office *should* be closed, but that doesn't mean it actually *is* closed. Perhaps a violation has occurred. So, whether the branch office is closed is unknown.

[42] Example also from "SBVR Support for Inference: Logical Effects of Claims of Necessity and Obligation on Implications"

Since behavioral rules don't produce inferences, they don't 'chain' in the usual sense of that term either.

Uncertainty

Behavioral rules are about coordinating groups and communities of people, not reasoning per se. Reasoning involving degree of certainty (as in expert systems such as MYCIN or in fuzzy logic) is a different problem space.

For example, an inference rule could be specified indicating that .96 is the likelihood of branch offices being closed between 1AM and 5AM. That rule, however, serves for reasoning, not supporting policy and detecting and reacting to violations.

Machine learning models make assessments with varying levels of certainty. What level of certainty is desirable or required is a matter of concern. Such thresholds could be expressed by rules. Whether such threshold rules are technical or communal (i.e., subject to business governance) should be considered carefully, most likely on a case-by-case basis.

Glossary

The following conventions are followed for expressing the examples:

- Concepts, facts and rules (meanings) appear in *italics*.
- Designations, wordings and definitions appear in 'single quotes'.
- Sentences appear in "double quotes."

The basis for a definition is indicated explicitly if from *Merriam-Webster Unabridged Dictionary* (MWUD), the OMG specification SBVR (*Semantics of Business Vocabulary and Business Rules*),[43] or elsewhere.

[43] For terms with a basis in the OMG specification SBVR, an exact mapping is presented in the Glossary of *Business Knowledge Blueprints: Enabling Your Data to Speak the Language of the Business* (2nd ed), by Ronald G. Ross, 2020.

Term	Definition	Example(s)	Note(s)	Basis
accommodation [rules]	expressing **elements of guidance** explicitly and fully so as to avoid **conflicts**	General Access Rule: *A customer <u>that is not a gold customer</u> may have access to the warehouse only during regular business hours.* Gold Customer Access Rule: *A gold customer must be allowed access to the warehouse at all hours.* The former **rule statement** has been expressed so as to avoid a **conflict** with the latter **rule statement**.	1. An **element of guidance** whose meaning conflicts with some other **element(s) of guidance** must be taken that way; if no **conflict** is intended, the **element(s) of guidance** must be expressed in such a way as to avoid the **conflict**. 2. See also **face-value trustworthy [rules]**.	*SBVR – The Accommodation Principle*
activation [rules]	making some **element(s) of guidance** officially part of the current in-practice **body of guidance**		1. At the time of **activation**, the entire **guidance knowledgebase (rulebook)** should be free of **conflicts** and **ambiguity**. 2. Time of **activation** should not be confused with time of application, any event when **elements of guidance** are actually applied to evaluate a set of circumstances. 3. **Activation** does not assume an **element of guidance** is automatable.	
ambiguity	the condition of admitting of two or more meanings, of being understood in more than one way, or of referring to two or more **things** at the same time; looseness of signification or reference	"The chicken is ready to eat." Is the chicken ready to do the eating, or ready to be the object of eating? Which of the following does 'pool' mean? *swimming pool, car pool, the game played on a pool table, betting pool*	**Ambiguity** arises when there is more than one possible **interpretation** of an expression.	*taken directly from MWUD 2a(1) and (2)*
anomaly	something irregular or abnormal		If something is anomalous, it exhibits or contains incongruous or often contradictory elements. MWUD [anomalous] 3b	*MWUD 3*

Term	Definition	Example(s)	Note(s)	Basis
applicability condition	a criterion under which a **behavioral rule** has a different **enforcement level, violation response(s)**, and/or **guidance message(s)**	For the **rule**: *no-shirt, no-service* **applicability condition:** *lunch time on Friday and Saturday* **enforcement level:** *guideline* **applicability condition:** *all other times* **enforcement level:** strictly enforced	**Applicability conditions** permit highly-nuanced responses to violations – that is, situational sensitivity and situational awareness.	
authorization	an explicit **permission** by some authority that gives validity to the acts of some persons or agents that otherwise would be prohibited	For the **rule**: *No person is to make a payment from the company's accounts if the person is not authorized explicitly.* **authorization:** *Jane Smith is permitted to make a payment from the company's accounts* **authorization:** *Any senior manager is permitted to make a payment from the company's accounts.*	1. **Authorizations** involve use of resources that are deemed especially sensitive, dangerous, scarce, privileged, and/or valuable. 2. **Authorizations** require expressing a **prohibition** to act as an **exclusion zone**.	*SBVR*
behavioral rule	a **rule** that is an **obligation** or **prohibition**	*All drivers must stop for a red light.*	1. Contrast with **definitional rule**. 2. Unlike **definitional rules**, **behavioral rules** can be violated. 3. The purpose of **behavioral rules** is to shape (govern) day-to-day **business** activity and thereby to prevent undesirable situations (states of affairs).	*SBVR*
block-out [rules]	an **anomaly** in which two or more **rules** cannot be mutually satisfied in some situations because in those situations they are unintentionally in direct contradiction	*1. A shipment must include at least 3 orders.* *2. An out-of-state shipment must not include more than 1 order.* Assuming both **rules** to be **face-value trustworthy**, any out-of-state shipment is disallowed (blocked-out).	**Block-outs** often represent unresolved 'exceptions'	

Term	Definition	Example(s)	Note(s)	Basis
body of guidance	a collection of **elements of guidance**, along with relevant **concepts**		1. Informally, a **rulebook**. 2. The SBVR term is 'body of shared guidance.' However, that term does not include **concepts** (as expressed by **definitions** and **definitional rules**). For both elements of guidance and **concepts** together, SBVR uses the term 'body of shared meanings.' 3. Also called a **guidance knowledgebase**.	
business	an enterprise with a mission, goals and objectives and the authority to establish strategy and policies for itself		1. '**Business**' in this sense includes non-profit organizations, government agencies, etc. 2. In a broad sense the purpose of all the discourse (specifically **formal messaging**, usually text) within a **business** is to marshal its unique (often deep) **business** knowledge to achieve its **business** goals and objectives.	
business policy	an element of business governance concerned with controlling or influencing the activity of a **business**	*Rental cars are not to be exported.*	A **business policy** is generally not practicable. Compared to a **rule**, a **business policy** tends to be: • less structured • less discrete or not atomic • less carefully expressed in terms of a standard **vocabulary**	*SBVR*
business rule	a **rule** that is **practicable** and that is under **business** jurisdiction		A **business rule** is always under **business** jurisdiction. For example, the laws of nature are not **business rules**. A provision of the tax code is not a **business rule** either; rather, your interpretation of it is.	*SBVR*

Term	Definition	Example(s)	Note(s)	Basis
business vocabulary	a **vocabulary** that is under the jurisdiction of a **business**, government or industry		1. A **business vocabulary** may be for a special area of business knowledge. 2. A **concept model** provides the basis for creating a robust **business vocabulary**.	*SBVR*
completeness [rules]	a set of **rules** being sufficient for the activity of interest		A set of **rules** is complete if no significant rules are missing (omitted).	
concept	a notion in a person's mind that is a unit of knowledge created by a unique combination of **definitional criteria**	your notion or the organization's shared notion of *customer*	A **concept** is communicated and shared based on its **definition** and/or expression of **definitional rule(s)**.	*SBVR*
concept model	a set of **concepts** structured according to the relations among them		1. A **concept model** provides a classification scheme for **things** of the **business**. 2. A **concept model** provides the basis for creating a robust **business vocabulary**. 3. A **concept model** is a linguistic blueprint, not a data model. 4. As a practical matter, a **concept model** is almost always represented by a **concept model diagram** along with **definitional criteria** expressed in a companion glossary. 5. A **concept model** expressed as an SBVR-style **business vocabulary** may be correctly understood as a business ontology.	*SBVR*
concept model diagram	a graphical representation of a **concept model**		Contrast with **concept model**.	

Term	Definition	Example(s)	Note(s)	Basis
conflict [rules]	an **anomaly** within or among some **rule(s)** such that multiple states or outcomes are required that cannot all be satisfied simultaneously	*1. A high-priced, fragile item must be picked up by the customer.* *2. A high-priced, fragile item must be shipped by an insured carrier.* It is impossible for an item to be picked up by a customer if it is shipped, and vice versa.	1. If some **rule(s)** are in **conflict**, they prescribe states of affairs that are mutually exclusive or contradictory. 2. The prevention, detection and elimination of **conflicts** are important activities in creating high-quality sets of **rules**.	
context	the **thing** that provides boundaries (scope) for the meaning of a **term**	For **conflict [rules]**, the **context** is **rules**. The word 'conflict' can have many other meanings.	A **term** establishing **context** for another **term** should always have a **definition** in the same **business vocabulary**.	*SBVR*
decision table	representation of a set of **inference rules** in a tabular form		Appropriate inclusion of an expression in a **decision table** automatically indicates the expression as a **rule**.	
declarative [statement]	constituting a statement that can be either true or false	"The sky is blue."		*MWUD 2*
definition	a phrase expressing the essential nature of a person or thing or class of persons or of things : an answer to the question "what is x?" or "what is an x?"	[any **definition** in this Glossary]	1. **Definitions** express **definitional criteria**. 2. A **definition** is not the same as a description that explains the role, function, purpose, usage, or relevance of something.	*based on MWUD 2*
definitional criterion	a **necessity** pertaining to a property of a **thing** that distinguishes the **thing** from other **things**	*Being warm-blooded and producing milk within the body to feed offspring* are definitional criteria of *mammal.*	1. **Definitional criteria** serve to classify **things**. They answer the question, 'What counts as an **instance** of this concept?' 2. **Definitional criteria** may be expressed by **definitions** and/or established by **definitional rules**.	

Term	Definition	Example(s)	Note(s)	Basis
definitional rule	a **rule** that establishes a **definitional criterion**	*A mammal always has hair.*	1. **Definitional rules** can be expressed either as parts of **definitions** or as separate statements. 2. Contrast with **behavioral rule**. Unlike **behavioral rules**, **definitional rules** cannot be violated. 3. SBVR treats **definitional rules** as expansions of **definitions**, making no distinction under the covers between them.	*SBVR*
disambiguation	the act of establishing a single interpretation for a **textual business statement**	"We mean 'pool [swimming]', not any of the following: • 'pool [commuting]' • 'pool [table games]' • 'pool [betting]'."		*based on MWUD [disambiguate]*
element of guidance	a guide for conduct or action; one of a set of usually official regulations by which an activity (as a sport) is governed; a standard on which a decision or judgment may be based	*the infield fly rule in baseball* *any of the rules of professional basketball*	1. A collection of **elements of guidance** is called a **body of guidance**. 2. **Elements of guidance** include **rules**, **permissions**, **authorizations**, **rights**, **warranties**, etc. **Business policies** are also considered **elements of guidance**.	*taken directly from MWUD [rule] 1a, 1f and [criterion] 2* *SBVR*

Term	Definition	Example(s)	Note(s)	Basis
enforcement level	how strictly a **behavioral rule** is to be enforced	For the **rule**: *A high-risk customer must not place a rush order.* **enforcement level**: *strictly enforced*	1. The **enforcement level** for any given **rule** is always completely independent of the logic expressed by that **rule**. That way, either can be changed on its own at any time. 2. 'Guideline' is the least restrictive of all **enforcement levels** (no sanction of any kind for violation). 3. SBVR does not standardize **enforcement levels** per se, leaving that matter to platform implementers. It does, however, provide the necessary underpinning.	*SBVR*
exception [rules]	a foreseen, explicit set of circumstances in which different-than-normal guidance is to be followed	*Seeing-eye dogs as an exception to dogs not being allowed in a hospital.*	Unforeseen 'exceptions' are handled by appropriate **enforcement level**. They require injection of sentiment, human discretion, and common sense.	
exclusion zone	a **prohibition** on something that can be overcome by explicit prior **permissions**	*No person is to make a payment from the company's accounts if the person is not authorized explicitly.*	A **permission** that overcomes an **exclusion zone** is an **authorization**.	*SBVR – 'dark area'*
face-value trustworthy [rules]	being able to trust exactly what the statement of a **rule** expresses, whatever is right in front of the reader		1. An **element of guidance** means only exactly what it says, so it must say everything it means. 2. Since all **rules** depend on **definitions** of **terms** and **definitional rules**, this principle assumes the **vocabulary** is familiar or accessible to the reader. 3. See also **accommodation [rules]**.	*SBVR – The Wholeness Principle*

Term	Definition	Example(s)	Note(s)	Basis
fact	a **proposition** that is taken to be true	*The Eiffel Tower is located in Paris.*	1. A **fact** is always expressed as a **declarative** sentence that is not a paradox. 2. Data stored in an information/record-keeping system (e.g., a database) is intended to represent **facts**.	*SBVR*
fact acquisition question	a question posed to obtain some fact needed to evaluate a rule	For the **rule**: *no shirt, no service* **fact acquisition question:** *Is this person wearing a shirt?*	To convert a well-expressed **rule** to some **fact acquisition question(s)** is generally straightforward.	
flash point	a real-time event in **business** activity that attempts to change a **state of affairs** relevant to one or more **rules**	For the **rule**: *A customer must be assigned to an agent if the customer has placed an order.* **flash points:** - When a customer places an order - When an agent leaves the company	1. **Flash points** for **definitional rules** often act as extended flash points for **behavioral rules**. 2. Evaluation of **flash points** for sets of **inference rules** (as in **decision tables**) is often deferred so as to optimize **operational business decisions**.	
flash-time message	a **guidance message** intended to be disseminated immediately upon evaluation of some rule at a flash point	For the **rule**: *A reservation must indicate an intended pick-up branch.* **flash-time message:** *We need to know where you'd like to pick up your rental car.*	1. **Flash-time messages** are often but not always associated with attempted violations of **behavioral rules**. 2. Contrast with **pre-posted message**.	
formal communication	*See* **formal messaging**.			
formal messaging	communicating in writing to convey knowledge among people who are not face-to-face or directly connected in real time and who do not share an obvious **context**	*[Almost any text in this book.]*	1. **Formal messaging** cannot depend on body language, verbal cues, or an implicit setting or objective to establish **context**. 2. Contrast with **informal messaging**.	

Term	Definition	Example(s)	Note(s)	Basis
guidance knowledgebase	*See* **body of guidance**.			
guidance message	an additional message associated with a **rule** and its **rule statement(s)**	For the **rule** *no shirt, no service:* **guidance message:** "We'd be pleased to offer you a low-cost t-shirt you can take with you after you dine."	1. A **guidance message** can clarify a **rule**, indicate the **rule's** motivation, tutor participants, or provide some solution(s). 2. Refer to **flash-time message** and **pre-posted message**.	
impossibility	a **necessity** that a **thing** cannot be classified a certain way	*It is impossible for a* **thing** *that does not have sleeves to be a shirt. A* **thing** *is not a shirt if it has no sleeves.*	Contrast with **necessity**.	*SBVR*
incompleteness [rules]	*See* **completeness [rules]**.			
inference rule	*See* **logical implication**.			
informal communication	*See* **informal messaging**.			
informal messaging	communicating among people who are face-to-face or directly connected more or less in real time or share an obvious **context**		1. **Informal messaging** can depend on body language, verbal cues, and an implicit setting or joint objective to establish **context**. 2. Contrast with **formal messaging**.	

Term	Definition	Example(s)	Note(s)	Basis
instance	a **thing** to which a **concept** corresponds	A. The **thing** called the 'Eiffel Tower.' B. The place called 'Canada.' C. The person called 'Isaac Newton.'	1. **Concept models** always treat an **instance** as being in the universe of discourse. A value of a field or data type in a stored database or file is *not* an **instance**. What's in a database or file merely *represents* **instances**. Similarly, the name of an **instance** merely *represents* the **instance**. 2. An **instance** of a **concept** can always be taken as an example of that **concept**.	*SBVR*
instruction	a direction or order; detailed information telling how something should be done, operated, or assembled	"Wait until your name is called, then come to the desk."	1. **Instructions** indicate something to do (or not), usually coming in meaningful sequences. 2. **Instructions** are about doing the right **things**; **rules** are about ensuring the right results. 3. Contrast with **rule**.	*Oxford Languages 1 & 2*
interpretation	the act of clarifying what is not immediately plain or explicit in a **textual business statement**; that is, resolving **ambiguity**		**Interpretation** effectively means resolving **ambiguity** beyond reasonable doubt.	*based on MWUD 1a*
knock-out rule	a **behavioral rule** set up to pre-empt the result of some inference rules in special cases	A **rule** to ensure an underage applicant or felon never has their mortgage application approved no matter how good their other credentials.	A **knock-out rule** excludes specific cases from 'normal' treatment as specified by some decision logic as a matter of **business policy**, perhaps because the results would otherwise be unfair, unseemly, high-risk, or perverse.	

Term	Definition	Example(s)	Note(s)	Basis
legal obligation	an **obligation** that derives from: a) a contract (through its explicit or implicit terms); b) legislation; or c) other operation of law			*International Financial Reporting Standards (IFRS)*
level of enforcement	*See* **enforcement level**.			
logical implication	a logical relationship of the form symbolically rendered "if p then strictly q" in which q is deducible from p	*it is raining → streets are wet* *Usage is on a weekend during peak hours AND usage is for more than 2 hours → fee is $15.*	1. **Logical implications** imply new **facts** from existing **facts**, able to support what is commonly called inference. 2. **Logical implications** are used for **reasoning**.	*MWUD 2b(2)*
modality [rules]	a way in which one might think of the truth of a **proposition**, or of the social desirability of act(s) being performed that would make the **proposition** true	**necessity** **impossibility** **obligation** **prohibition** **permission**		*SBVR*
necessity	a constraint on classifying **things**	*A shirt covers the chest. A* ***thing*** *is not a shirt if it does not cover the chest.*	1. A **necessity** is given by a **definition** or **definitional rule**. 2. Contrast with **obligation**.	*SBVR*
noun concept	a **concept** that is the meaning of a noun or noun phrase	your notion or the organization's shared notion of *customer*	Contrast with **verb concept**.	*SBVR*

Term	Definition	Example(s)	Note(s)	Basis
obligation	an organizational, legal, or social constraint on behavior	*A shirt is required to enter and dine in this restaurant.*	1. A **behavioral rule** is an **obligation**. 2. Behavior includes conduct, action, practice, and procedure. 3. Contrast with **necessity**.	*SBVR*
operational business decision	a decision that · pertains to groups and communities of people · occurs repetitively in everyday activity · can be based on explicit **inference rules**, especially in **decision tables**	*Should this insurance claim be accepted, rejected, or examined for fraud?* *Which resource should be assigned to this task?* *Which service should be used to ship this package?*	**Knock-out rules** are directly relevant to **operational business decisions**.	
optimistic world	anything being permitted unless expressly prohibited		1. An **optimistic world** is the default assumption for **rules**. 2. An **optimistic world** is not prudent concerning use of, and/or access to, resources that are deemed especially sensitive, dangerous, scarce, privileged, and/or valuable. 3. Contrast with **pessimistic world**.	*SBVR – 'light world'*
permission	an acknowledgement that certain behavior is allowed	*A person of any age is permitted to hold a bank account.*	1. A **permission** implies consent, not entitlement. Contrast with **right**. 2. A **prohibition** 'wins' over a **permission** for the same **state of affairs**. 3. Contrast with **rule**. 4. Contrast with **authorization**.	*SBVR – 'advice of permission'*

Term	Definition	Example(s)	Note(s)	Basis
pessimistic world	everything being prohibited unless expressly permitted		1. **Authorizations** require declaring an explicit **exclusion zone** in which something is prohibited unless expressly authorized (creating a selective **pessimistic world**). 2. Contrast with **optimistic world**. 3. **Pessimistic worlds** can also be established for possibilities – i.e., anything not expressly specified as possible is assumed impossible. Such specifications would affect **definitions** and **definitional rules**, rather than behavior directly.	
policy	*See* **business policy.**			
practicable	being sufficiently detailed and precise that a person can apply it effectively and consistently in relevant circumstances to know what behavior is or is not acceptable, or to know what **things** a **concept** corresponds to		1. Assuming a person knows the *business vocabulary*, or has access to it, the person should be able to read any *practicable* statement and be able to fully understand it without external clarification. 2. This notion originated in the Business Rule Group's *Business Motivation Model* (BMM), which like SBVR, is also an OMG specification.	*SBVR*
pre-posted message	a **guidance message** that is pre-emptive in the sense it warns that a rule applies and might be enforced	*No shirt, no service* at the entrance to a restaurant. *No Trespassing!* on a fence line.	Contrast with **flash-time message**.	
prohibition	an **obligation** to avoid certain behavior	*No vehicles in the park.*	1. A **prohibition** is an **obligation** to avoid a certain behavior. 2. Contrast with **obligation**.	*SBVR*

Term	Definition	Example(s)	Note(s)	Basis
proposition	the meaning of a **declarative** sentence	*The sky is blue.*	1. The sentence cannot express a paradox. Also, the meaning of a **proposition** is invariant through all the paraphrases and translations of any sentence that expresses it. 2. A **proposition** corresponds to a **state of affairs**. 3. Contrast with **state of affairs**.	*SBVR*
reasoning	evaluating **rules** to logically infer factual conclusions from other **facts**			
right [rules]	an entitlement to something	*freedom of speech* *protection against forced self-incrimination*	1. In groups and communities of people, every **behavioral rule** has a companion **right** (even if never articulated). 2. In contracts, a duty (**obligation**) for one party translates to a **right** for the other party. 3. Contrast with **permission**.	
rule	a specific **obligation** or **necessity**	*No shirt, no service.* *No vehicles in the park.* *A mammal always has hair.*	1. A **rule** always tends to narrow options or possibilities, thereby removing some degree of freedom. A rule is always a constraint. 2. A **rule** can either be a **definitional rule** or a **behavioral rule**. How much freedom a **behavioral rule** removes depends on **enforcement level**. 3. To be useful, a rule should be **practicable**. 4. A **rule** should never call for the execution of an action. A **rule** is not a command or instruction. 5. Contrast with **business policy**. 6. Contrast with **rule statement**. 7. Contrast with **permission**.	*SBVR, which defines:* *rule:* proposition that obligates a given state of affairs or that necessitates a given state of affairs

Term	Definition	Example(s)	Note(s)	Basis
rulebook	*Refer to* **body of guidance.**		Real-world **rulebooks** for games, etc. generally include **permissions**, **rights**, etc. So, use of the term '**rulebook**' tends to be a bit loose.	
rule platform	a software platform responsible for the **activation** and evaluation of **elements of guidance**			
rule statement	a statement that expresses the meaning of a **rule**		1. The same **rule** can be expressed in more than one way, and in multiple natural languages. 2. Contrast with **rule**.	
state of affairs	situation or circumstance		1. A **state of affairs** can be possible (a rainy day) or impossible (a unicorn galloping across a glen). 2. Contrast with **proposition**. A **proposition** is either true or false. A **state of affairs**, in contrast, either occurs or does not occur.	*SBVR*
structured business vocabulary	a **business vocabulary** that is based on a **concept model**			
subsumption [rules]	an **anomaly** among **rule(s)** that all require or disallow the same state, except that one **rule** requires or disallows the state for a broader set of circumstances than the other **rule**	Rule 1. *A rush order must have a destination.* Rule 2. *An order must have a destination.* The first **rule** is subsumed by the second **rule** and therefore should be eliminated.	1. A **rule** is subsumed by some other **rule** if the other **rule** covers all possible circumstances and more where the former **rule** might need to be evaluated. 2. **Subsumption** can be considered a form of redundancy. 3. Prevention, detection, and elimination of **subsumptions** are important activities in creating high-quality sets of **rules**.	

Term	Definition	Example(s)	Note(s)	Basis
term	a designation for a general **concept**	A. 'tower' B. 'nation' C. 'scientist'	1. In the everyday sense, a **term** is a word or expression that has a precisely limited meaning in some uses or is peculiar to a science, art, profession, trade, or special subject [MWUD 8a]. 2. Use of a **term** sometimes needs to be qualified by **context** to be unambiguous.	*SBVR*
textual business statement	any textual expression, apart from simply a **term**, name, or **wording**, created for communicating about some **business** matter	1. The command to a bot, "Turn on the lights." 2. The **rule**: "A library card may be used to check-out a book only if the book is owned by a library for which the card is authorized." 3. A statement in a contract, product/service specification, or governance or regulatory compliance document. 4. A monthly sales report	1. To communicate as unambiguously as possible, a **textual business statement** should be fully based on a **structured business vocabulary**. 2. Both structured data and written **business** communications ('unstructured data') are **textual business statements**. 3. For the sake of convenience, a question is also considered a **textual business statement**. 4. A **textual business statement** can include an arbitrary number of sentences or sentence fragments. 5. A statement in a programming language is not considered a **textual business statement**.	*taken directly from MWUD [statement] 2: something stated: as a report or narrative (as of facts, events, or opinions)*
thing	anything perceivable or conceivable		A **thing** can be a physical **thing** or a **thing** in the mind (e.g., a **concept** or meaning). It can also be an expression.	*SBVR*
unintended block-out	*See* block-out [rules].			

Term	Definition	Example(s)	Note(s)	Basis
verb concept	the meaning of a verb phrase (including optional prepositions) along with one or more **noun concepts** in specific relation to that verb phrase	What is meant by either of the **wordings**, 'person owns vehicle' or 'vehicle is owned by person'.	1. Implicitly or explicitly, the **noun concept(s)** in a **verb concept** is/are included as **verb-based roles**. 2. In **concept models**, **verb concepts** can be **unary**, **binary**, or **n-ary**.	*SBVR*
verb concept wording	*See* **wording**.			
violation response	a special action, process, or procedure that can be invoked to avoid, mitigate, sanction, or compensate for the detected violation of a **behavioral rule**	For the **rule**: *no-shirt, no-service* **violation response:** Offer a discount coupon as an enticement for a future visit.	1. **Violation responses** should occur in real time if possible and generally aim at mitigating risks or seizing opportunities. 2. Examples include posting of penalties or incentives, special messages or displays (e.g., an alarm, warning light, etc.), scheduling an event (e.g., a review to ensure the problem is resolved), enforcement of other **rules**, etc.	
vocabulary	a list or collection of words and phrases and their **definitions** and/or **definitional rules**	[the collection of **terms** in this Glossary]	1. A **vocabulary** should include both **terms** and **wordings**. 2. See also **business vocabulary**. 3. See also **structured business vocabulary**.	*based on MWUD 1* *SBVR*
wording	an expression (usually words) that provides a syntactic structure or pattern that represents a **verb concept**	The sentence "A person who owns a car can never steal the car." is based on the **wordings** 'person owns car' and 'person steals car'.	In English, a **wording** always includes an explicit verb and/or preposition.	*SBVR*

INDEX

A

accommodation, 252, 258
actions, 63–64, 66
  and inferences, 20–21
  and states, 17–19
  vs. rules, 17–21, 193
activation, 179, 252, 266
  vs. application of guidance, 194–195
activity scenarios, 144
AI. *See* Artificial Intelligence (AI)
ambiguity, 53, 67, 79–85, 162, 167–168, 194, 252, 261
anomalies, 123, 135–136, 153, 252–253, 256, 266
  and automated tools, 196
  conflicts, 137–138
  in guidance, 194–195
  incompleteness, 143–145
  redundancy, 140–143
  subsumption, 138–140
applicability conditions, 36, 42–44, 127, 153, 223–224, 253
Artificial Intelligence (AI), 59, 185, 204
assumed computations, 93–94, 96, 121
authorizations, 128–129, 153, 155, 181, 253, 257, 258, 263–264
  exclusion zones and, 167–169
  optimistic *vs.* pessimistic world, 166–167
  permissions and prohibitions, 165–166
  specifying, 169–171
  vs. violation responses, 171
automation, 59–60, 186, 196
auxiliary verb, 22–23

B

behavioral rules, 25, 28–30, 51, 253, 257–259, 261, 263, 265, 268
  delayed evaluations, 238–239
  and flash points, 100–108
  and logical implication, 248–249
  real-time evaluation, 237–239
  and rights, 173–174
  statements, 231
  Rule Messaging Triad for, 118–120
  violations of, 35–44
  vs. definitional rules, 26–28, 48
block-outs, 138, 253, 267
BMM. *See* Business Motivation Model (BMM)
body of guidance, 156, 160–162, 182, 194–195, 212, 252, 254, 257, 260, 266
business, 254
business governance, 82, 125
business knowledge, 85
Business Motivation Model (BMM), 264
business policy, 32, 254, 257, 261, 265
business rule, 254
business vocabulary, 58, 76, 87, 134, 254–256, 266, 268
  developing, 91–93, 121
  structured, 23, 79, 88, 92, 121, 185, 266–268
by government rules, 11

C

categories, 130–131, 139–140
change, 188
commands, 65–66
community, and rules, 10
completeness, 16, 57, 77, 196, 255
  context, 73–75
  definitions *vs.* definitional rules, 76–77
  incompleteness, 143–145, 153, 260
  modifiers and qualifications, 75–76
compliance confirmation, 215
compliance reward, 215
computations, 93–94, 96, 121
concept model diagram, 71, 83, 92–94, 104–106, 118, 181, 191–192, 241

concept models, 23, 81, 83, 88, 92, 185, 255, 261, 266
data models, 210
finding flash points, 104
higher-order expressions, 209
intensions and extensions, 207–208
ontologies, 208–209
concepts, 254, 255, 261–262
and rules, 14
conditional definitional rules
and logical implication, 247–248
conditional instructions, 65–66, 227
conflicts, 132–133, 153, 252, 256
among modal operators, 212–213
among rules and permissions, 161–162
unintended block-outs, 138
vocabulary, 137
context, 41, 58, 69, 73–75, 83, 87, 92, 110, 112, 122, 133–134, 167, 185, 196, 256, 259, 260, 267
contracts
and agreements, 25
and rights, 178–179
contractual obligations, 89
controlled vocabulary, 23
corporate memory, 82, 188
CRUD (create, retrieve, update, delete) words, 29, 64, 236
customer experience, and rules, 13–14

D

data, 229–230
models, 210
and rules, 16
data quality, 3, 16, 40, 67, 102–104, 121, 166, 183, 243–244
decision tables, 21, 128, 140, 196, 197–198, 224, 256, 259, 263
and exceptions, 147–152
fact acquisition questions, 200–201
factual expressions into, 69
guidance messages, 201
rule statements, 199–200
and *Rule Messaging Triad*, 117, 199
decisions, 21, 203–205, 239
DecisionSpeak, 204
declarative statement, 61–66, 87, 104, 136, 192, 209, 234, 256, 259, 265
definition, 30–32, 208, 254–256, 258
and logical implication, 246
and rights, 174–175
vs. definitional rules, 32, 48, 56, 76–77, 87, 132
definitional criterion, 14, 71, 114, 137, 162, 175, 192, 243, 246, 255–257
definitional rules, 25, 30–33, 45–49, 51, 116, 253–259, 262, 264–265, 268
delayed evaluations, 238–239
and flash points, 102, 237–239
and logical implication, 246–247
real-time evaluation, 237–239
statements, 232
Rule Messaging Triad for, 116–117
vs. behavioral rules, 26–28, 48
vs. definitions, 32, 48, 56, 76–77, 87, 132
delayed evaluations, 238–239
Description Logic (DL), 208
disambiguation, 79–85, 88, 185, 257
DL. *See* Description Logic (DL)
do's and don'ts messages, 109–110, 121

E

edge cases, 144
elements of guidance, 156, 161, 163, 176, 181–182, 193, 195, 198, 252, 254, 257–258, 266
embedded computations, 93–94, 96, 121
enforcement level, 28, 36, 39–40, 43, 126–127, 137–138, 153, 159, 162, 171, 217–219, 223, 253, 258, 262, 265
event detection, 242–243
event management, 244
exceptions, 121, 123, 258
applicability conditions, 127
authorizations, 128–129
enforcement level, 126–127
handling, 97–99, 129–133
knock-out rules, 128
unforeseen, 129, 258
exclusion zones, 167–172, 253, 258, 264
existing facts (stored data), 75
explicit permissions, 160

explicit rules, 15
explicit wordings, 84
expressing knowledge of states, 21–23

F

face-value trustworthy, 131–134, 138, 154, 160, 161, 176, 222, 252, 253, 258
fact, 87, 259
  about, 67–68
  and concepts, 70–71
  and data, 229–230
  expressing rules, 71–72
  vs. rules, 68–70
fact acquisition question(s), 113–120, 122, 200–201, 259
factual expressions, 67, 87, 114, 191
First Order Logic (FOL), 208
flash points, 89, 111, 121, 144, 162, 243, 259
  and behavioral rules, 100–108
  and definitional rules, 102, 237–239
  examples, 103–107
  and WHEN expression, 234
flash-time messages, 111–112, 259–260, 264
FOL. *See* First Order Logic (FOL)
formal communication, 58, 74–75, 79–80, 91, 110, 133, 225, 259
formal messaging, 80–81, 254, 259, 260
formal statement, 112, 122
freedom of speech, 174–175

G

governance
  gap, 186–187
  and rules, 10–11
government, and rules, 11
guidance, 20, 55, 79
  anomalies in, 194
  application/activation of, 194
  logical consistency of, 42
guidance knowledgebase (rulebook), 20, 42, 134, 156, 160, 169, 193, 194, 252, 254, 260
guidance message(s), 36, 40–41, 115–120, 122, 160, 199, 201, 215, 218, 223, 253, 259, 260, 264
  flash-time messages, 111–112
  pre-posted messages, 112–113
guidelines, 39

H

'hidden hands', 130–131, 154
hidden priority schemes, 130
hidden semantics, 62–63
high-level guidance, 56
high-quality rules, 135, 153, 256, 266
higher-order expressions, 209

I

IF-THEN syntax, 224–228
impossibility, 32, 157, 211, 232, 260, 262
in government rules, 11
incompleteness, 143–145, 153, 260
inference rules, 14–15, 20, 26, 107, 147–152, 153, 193–194, 197, 199–200, 203–205, 223–225, 237, 239, 249, 256, 259, 260, 263
inferences, 20–21
informal communication, 74, 109, 260
informal messaging, 83, 112, 259, 260
informal vs. formal communication, 133–134
innovation, and rules, 11–12
instance, 27, 45, 51, 175, 203, 207, 216, 256, 261
instruction, 20–21, 62–64, 67, 109–110, 111, 261, 265
  conditional, 65–66, 227
interpretation, 32, 80, 82, 121, 261
  developing business vocabulary, 91–93, 121
  embedded computations, 93–94, 96
  exceptions, 97–99
  thresholds, 96–97

K

key performance indicators (KPIs), 45
knock-out rules, 123, 128, 153, 194, 205, 261, 263
  pre-empting inference rules, 151–152
  stage setting, 147–151
knowledge
  expressing, 21–23

and rules, 9
KPIs. *See* key performance indicators (KPIs)

L

law and contracts, 174
legal obligation, 1, 28, 89, 173, 178, 201, 212, 221, 231, 253, 262–265
level of enforcement. *See* enforcement level
linguistic equivalence, 140–141
logical consistency, 20, 42, 66, 135, 174
  activation *vs.* application of guidance, 194–195
  automated consistency checking, 196
  discovering anomalies in guidance, 195
  rules *vs.* actions, 193
logical implication, 15, 171, 198, 226–227, 237, 245–249, 260, 262. *See also* inference rules

M

machine learning (ML), 15, 59, 185, 203, 249
material implication, 226
messages, 89, 121
  behavioral rules *Rule Messaging Triad*, 118–120
  definitional rules *Rule Messaging Triad*, 116–117
  do's and don'ts, 109–110
  Rule Messaging Triad, 112–120, 122, 200–201, 259
ML. *See* machine learning (ML)
modal equivalence, 142
modality, 70, 161, 209, 211–213, 262
modifiers, 75–76
motivation, 48

N

natural language processing (NLP), 196
natural languages, 22, 59, 114, 184–186
  ANDs and ORs in, 79
near identicals, 142
necessity, 32, 49, 157, 211, 232, 260, 262
NLP. *See* natural language processing (NLP)
noun concepts, 71, 84, 92, 181, 191, 192, 241, 262, 268

O

obligation, 28, 231, 253, 262– 265
ontologies, 208–209
operational business decisions, 15, 21, 194, 197, 204–205, 239, 241, 243, 259, 263
optimistic world, 171, 212, 263, 264
  vs. pessimistic world, 166–167
over specialization, 139
overabundance, 126
OWL. *See* Web Ontology Language (OWL)

P

pattern questions, 143
permission, 144, 155, 157, 181, 253, 257, 258, 262–263, 265
  expressing, 160–161
  and prohibitions, 165–166
  retaining explicit, 159–160
  vs. guideline/suggestion, 162
  vs. rights, 175–177
  vs. rule, 158–159, 161–162
pessimistic world, 168, 172, 212, 263–264
  vs. optimistic world, 166–167
policies and rules, 10–11, 52, 89
  See also business policy
positive reinforcement, 163, 215–216
potential violation. *See* flash points
practicability, 33, 55–57, 87, 91, 111, 121, 131, 176, 254, 264–265
  automation, 59–60
  gold standard, 57–59
pre-posted messages, 112–113, 259–260, 264
precision, 77
preemptive rule, 131
procedure, 62–64
processes, 63–64
programmer workload, 107, 183, 241–242
  event detection, 242–243
  event management, 244

prohibition, 28–29, 142, 157, 161, 168, 173, 195, 231, 253, 258, 262–264
  and permission, 165–166
proposition, 67, 211, 259, 262, 265–266

Q

qualifications, 75–76

R

real-time evaluation, 237–239
reasoning, 29–30, 32, 249, 262, 265
redundancy, 140–143, 153
regulations, 89
requirements, 3
  and rules, 15–16
restricted permission, 142, 231
restricted possibility, 232
'reversal' equivalence, 141–142
rewards, 37, 102, 120, 215–216
rights, 25, 257, 265
  authorizations, permissions, and, 155–156, 181–182
  and behavioral rules, 173–174
  and contracts, 178–179
  declaring, 177–178
  and definitions, 174–175
  vs. permission, 175–177
risks, and rules, 9
Rule Messaging Triad, 115–116, 122
  for behavioral rules, 118–120
  and decision tables, 117, 199
  for definitional rules, 116–117
  fact acquisition question(s), 113–120, 122, 200–201, 259
  formal statement, 112, 122, 199–200
  guidance message(s), 116–120, 122, 201
rule of law, 55
rule platforms, 59, 102, 104, 107, 152, 183–189, 193, 234, 241, 244, 266
rule statements, 11, 36, 53, 72, 111, 123, 132–134, 138, 154, 185, 199–200, 225, 227, 234, 252, 260, 265, 266
rulebook, 20, 42, 134, 156, 160, 169, 193–194, 252, 254, 260, 266
rules, 255, 257–258, 263, 265
  actions, and inferences, 20–21
  applying, 19–20
  expressing knowledge of states, 21–23
  and risks, 9
  states, and actions, 17–19
RuleSpeak®, 69, 81

S

sanction, 28
SBVR. *See* Semantics of Business Vocabulary and Business Rules (SBVR)
self-incrimination, 175
Semantics of Business Vocabulary and Business Rules (SBVR), 5, 69, 192, 207, 211, 231, 251
state of affairs, 18, 64, 157, 166, 175, 193, 211–212, 221, 231–232, 237, 253, 256, 259, 263, 265–266
states, 17–19
  and actions, 17–19
  expressing knowledge, 21–23
stored data, 75
strategy, and rules, 12–13
structured business vocabulary, 20, 23, 79, 88, 92, 121, 136, 145, 160, 169, 185, 193, 266–268
structured data, 230
subject matter experts, 59, 64, 85, 121
subsumption, 138–140, 153, 266

T

term, 14, 76, 111, 245–246, 267
terms and conditions, 49
test scenarios, 144
textual business statement, 69, 245, 257, 261, 267
thresholds, 96–97, 121, 144
traceability, 56, 82, 187

U

unambiguity, 79–85
unary verb concepts, 84
uncertainty, 249
undesirable states, 19
unforeseen exceptions, 129, 258
unintended block-outs, 138, 267
unresolved violations, 44
unsuccessful actions, 18

V
verb concepts, 21–22, 71, 84–85, 92–93, 105, 182, 191–192, 241, 262, 268
violation response(s), 36, 41–42, 162–163, 171, 183, 193, 215, 222–223, 253, 268
violations, 29, 35–36, 101, 120, 159
  applicability conditions, 42–44
  detecting, 36–39, 59
  enforcement levels, 39–40
  guidance message, 40–41
  responses, 41–42
  unresolved, 44
vocabulary, 104, 106, 118, 124, 136–137, 241, 254–256, 258, 268. *See also* business vocabulary

W
warranties, 156, 181, 221–222, 257
Web Ontology Language (OWL), 209
WHEN expression, 225, 233–234
wording, 84–85, 93, 251, 267, 268

Other recent books by Ronald G. Ross ...

Business Knowledge Blueprints:
Enabling Your Data to Speak the Language of the Business (2nd ed.)

The foundation and forerunner to *Rules: Shaping Behavior and Knowledge*. This authoritative book explains concept models and structured business vocabularies.

Use this book as a guide to creating shared understanding. It explains everything you need to know about:

- Developing business vocabularies
- Defining terms
- Creating concept structures

Business Rule Concepts: ***Getting to the Point of Knowledge (4th ed.)***

The classic in the field, this book is an easy-to-understand explanation of business rules and how they relate to business processes and business vocabulary.

Find out about kinds of business rules and how to make business processes smart and agile. Down-to-earth, highly informative.

Building Business Solutions: ***Business Analysis with Business Rules (2nd ed.)*** (with Gladys S.W. Lam)

How can you put the 'business' into business analysis? How do you deliver true business value? What should you be doing before requirements?

This handbook presents practical, proven, innovative methods to build great business solutions, then derive requirements directly from them.

Made in United States
North Haven, CT
21 February 2025

66121147R10157